Strategic Financial Management

for
Conferences,
Workshops,
and Meetings

Strategic Financial Management

for Conferences, Workshops, and Meetings

Robert G. Simerly

Jossey-Bass Publishers · San Francisco

Substantial discounts on bulk quantities of Jossey-Bass books are available to corporations, professional associations, and other organizations. For details and discount information, contact the special sales department at Jossey-Bass Inc., Publishers. (415) 433-1740; Fax (415) 433-0499.

For sales outside the United States, contact Maxwell Macmillan International Publishing Group, 866 Third Avenue, New York, New York 10022.

Manufactured in the United States of America

The paper used in this book is acid-free and meets the State of California requirements for recycled paper (50 percent recycled waste, including 10 percent postconsumer waste), which are the strictest guidelines for recycled paper currently in use in the United States.

The ink in this book is either soy- or vegetable-based and during the printing process emits fewer than half the volatile organic compounds (VOCs) emitted by petroleum-based ink.

Library of Congress Cataloging-in-Publication Data

Simerly, Robert.
  Strategic financial management for conferences, workshops, and meetings / Robert G. Simerly. — 1st ed.
      p. cm. — (A Joint publication in the Jossey-Bass higher and adult education series and the Jossey-Bass management series)
  Includes bibliographical references (p.   ) and index.
  1-55542-518-6
  1. Congresses and conventions—Finance—Handbooks, manuals, etc.
  2. Meetings—Finance—Handbooks, manuals, etc. I. Title.
  II. Series: Jossey-Bass higher and adult education series.
  III. Series: Jossey-Bass management series.
  AS6.S548 1992
  658.4′56—dc20   92-30631
                                                                          CIP

FIRST EDITION
HB Printing   10 9 8 7 6 5 4 3 2 1   *Code 9315*

A joint publication in
the Jossey-Bass
Higher and Adult Education Series
and
the Jossey-Bass
Management Series

Consulting Editor
Adult and Continuing Education

Alan B. Knox
University of Wisconsin, Madison

Contents

ix

Preface

This book shows how to design and implement a practical, easy-to-use strategic financial management system for any organization that plans conferences, workshops, and meetings. It is not necessary to be an accountant to understand and benefit from the strategies, guidelines, and suggestions presented. In fact, this book has been specifically written as a practical financial guide for the person who has never taken an accounting course but is interested in learning how better to manage the finances associated with conferences, workshops, and meetings.

This hands-on, practical guide has been written for busy professionals such as educational programmers in colleges and universities, training and development professionals, association executives, adult education specialists, and human resource development personnel, as well as for meeting and convention

planners, museum education and outreach staff, Cooperative
Extension programmers, leisure learning specialists, and staff
of governmental agencies—in short, for anyone employed in
an organization that plans conferences, workshops, and meetings. No matter how many programs you plan or what size your
organization is, this guide is designed to become an important
part of your professional library.

Overview of the Contents

Successful financial management rarely happens by accident.
Rather, it occurs as a result of careful and systematic planning
(Matkin, 1985; Garner, 1991). This book guides the reader
through easy-to-follow steps in the budgeting and strategic financial management process. Case studies that deal with real problems typically found in the busy, everyday world of those who
plan programs illustrate the practical nature of the suggestions
offered. Hints and guidelines for avoiding the most-often-made
mistakes are given to ensure success with strategic financial planning. It also includes suggestions for using personal computer
software to assist with financial management and sample budget
forms that can be easily adapted to meet the needs of any organization.

 It makes no difference how large or small your organization is or how many conferences, workshops, and meetings you
plan each year. This guide is designed to provide practical advice that can be implemented immediately.

 Chapter One begins with the basics, explaining how to
build a foundation for strategic financial management within
an organization and what the difference is between budgeting
and strategic financial management. Budgeting consists of the
process of creating documents (budgets) that are used to project
income and expenses. Strategic financial management is the
comprehensive process that develops specific strategies to ensure the overall financial health of a budget or series of budgets
over a period of time. Seven important characteristics of a strategic financial management system are identified so that readers
can incorporate these into their organizations. The chapter

concludes by presenting four rules for achieving success in strategic financial management and discussing the importance of establishing clear goals.

Chapter Two introduces five easy-to-follow steps for creating a budget for a single program, regardless of the size or type of the program. A case study illustrates these five steps and shows how to identify and classify all projected expenses for any program. The importance of always separating fixed and variable expenses is illustrated by a sample budget form that can be modified to fit the individual needs of any organization. This easy-to-use budget form becomes the basis for developing the sophisticated strategic financial process described in later chapters. Finally, the chapter offers hints for developing successful program budgets.

Chapter Three analyzes the importance of recovering administrative overhead for programs. A case study shows how to identify typical categories of general office overhead that can be used as the basis for planning an overhead budget for any type of organization. The basic steps for developing an administrative cost recovery system through the charging of administrative fees to individual programs are presented. The chapter concludes by offering practical tips for developing the general overhead budget.

Chapter Four introduces the basic methods for recovering administrative overhead: the flat administrative fee, the per person variable fee, the percentage of total expenses, and the combination method. A case study demonstrates how each of these methods can be used depending on the requirements of the sponsoring organization and its program. Using a case study with electronic spreadsheets for budgets, the chapter leads the reader through a step-by-step process illustrating exactly how to use each of these four types of recovery methods for administrative fees.

Chapter Five demonstrates how to develop an effective accounting system to enhance daily decision making. The chapter explains the difference between cash and accrual accounting and uses actual budgets to show why only accrual accounting should be used in planning conferences, workshops, and meetings. The chapter also illustrates how to set up an internal accounting system to track income and expenses for a department in a larger parent organization. Using a case study, the chapter shows how to establish an accrual accounting system, use encumbrances, and implement fund accounting.

Chapter Six uses a case study, with accompanying electronic spreadsheets, to illustrate the steps to developing a comprehensive strategic financial management system for a series of conferences, workshops, or meetings. The spreadsheets show how to create a financial planning model that projects income and expenses five years into the future. The chapter explains why organizations should develop this type of comprehensive strategic financial management process and how to avoid the most common mistakes.

Chapter Seven explains the strategy development process for handling financial management problems when projections indicate that income will not be enough to cover general overhead for an office. A case study illustrates the complex, constantly evolving process of strategic financial management and shows why it is crucial to develop specific courses of action to deal with problems as they arise. The suggestions offered serve as a useful road map for considering organizational change in relation to financial management.

Chapter Eight presents seven principles that can maximize success, enhance programs, and position an organization for long-term financial health. A central theme of the chapter is that strategic financial management enhances all forms of organizational planning. The chapter explains how to develop specific goals and objectives for a strategic financial management system and concludes by illustrating how strategic financial management can help enhance overall team management.

Chapter Nine identifies and analyzes important leadership skills needed for success in strategic financial management. At the top of the list of these important skills is the ability to manage ambiguity. Other important skills include the abilities to implement overall strategic long-range planning, to engage in environmental scanning, to manage conflict for productive results, to use computer software to engage in financial modeling, and to conduct sophisticated market research to develop comprehensive data-based marketing plans.

Resource A contains sample budget forms that can be modified to meet the needs of any organization. These budget forms are appropriate for any type of program, no matter what its size or complexity. Resource B is a convenient reference that summarizes the important financial management terms used throughout the book. Suggestions for choosing personal computer software helpful in achieving comprehensive strategic financial management are offered in Resource C.

Acknowledgments

I wish to thank the staff of the Division of Continuing Studies at the University of Nebraska, Lincoln. It is through the dedicated efforts of the entire administrative team that we have developed and refined many of the ideas on strategic financial management discussed in this book. The professionalism and dedication of the staff and its emphasis on excellent client service and financial management are always a source of inspiration to me.

I am especially grateful to my secretary, Dee Leonard, who has worked closely with me in producing this manuscript. It is a pleasure to work with such a highly skilled professional who has exhibited unlimited patience as we have worked through the many drafts of the manuscript.

Gale Erlandson, my editor at Jossey-Bass, has always provided helpful advice on clarifying ideas in the manuscript. I am also grateful to Alan Knox for his valuable editorial suggestions.

Finally, I wish to thank my wife, Coby Bunch Simerly. She is my colleague, best friend, and intellectual companion. I am always grateful for her assistance in providing helpful critiques of my many writing projects.

Lincoln, Nebraska   Robert G. Simerly
December 1992

The Author

Robert G. Simerly is dean of the Division of Continuing Studies and professor of adult and continuing education at the University of Nebraska, Lincoln. In this capacity, he provides the administrative leadership for a large continuing education organization with a staff of over 100 that serves 75,000 people each year in all 93 counties of Nebraska, all 50 states of the United States, and more than 125 countries. The Division of Continuing Studies operates one of the Kellogg continuing education centers, a comprehensive residential conference facility with a ninety-six-room hotel, a restaurant, and a wide variety of meeting rooms.

Simerly received his Ed.D. degree (1973) from the University of Tennessee, Knoxville, with a major in educational leadership and minors in industrial management and higher education. The author of numerous articles, Simerly has also written a number of books, including *Budgeting for Successful Conferences and Institutes* (1982), *Strategic Planning and Leadership in Continuing Education* (with associates, 1987), *Handbook of Marketing for Continuing Education* (with associates, 1989), and *Planning and Marketing Conferences and Workshops: Tips, Tools, and Techniques* (1990).

Simerly is an internationally known behavioral scientist who is particularly concerned with helping people to enhance their personal and organizational effectiveness. He believes that assisting people and organizations with their strategic planning is an effective method for achieving this goal.

Strategic Financial Management

for
Conferences,
Workshops,
and Meetings

1.

Developing a Foundation
for Strategic Financial Management

One of the main jobs of a leader is to create an
organizational climate that supports strategic
financial management.

Budgeting and strategic financial management are two very
different activities. Budgeting is an accounting activity that involves estimating income and expenses in an organization. Thus,
we speak of developing a yearly budget for an office that plans
and administers conferences, workshops, and meetings. We also
develop budgets for specific programs. However, budgets do
not necessarily represent the reality of what happens to money
in relation to a particular conference, workshop, or meeting.
A budget only represents a best judgment of what we project
income and expenses to be (Simerly, 1990a; Hildreth, 1990);
it does not ensure that the program will be a financial success.
Strategic financial management, on the other hand, is a
broader, more encompassing concept. Strategic financial management involves planning and managing a budget or a series

1

of budgets over an extended period of time to ensure the long-term financial security of an organization. When budgets for individual conferences, workshops, and meetings have been systematically planned and managed so that they break even over time, they become effective building blocks for an organization's long-range financial security.

The following short definitions help to distinguish between these two activities:

> *Budgeting:* the process of creating documents (budgets) that attempt to accurately project income and expenses for a program or series of programs
>
> *Strategic financial management:* the development of specific strategies to ensure the overall financial health of a budget or series of budgets over a period of time

By keeping these two definitions clearly in mind, you can analyze the time you devote to planning budgets and to strategic financial management. For example, try keeping a log for two weeks and writing down the amount of time you devote to budgeting versus the time you devote to strategic financial management. In many organizations, this type of time log can be very revealing. Because of the press of time in the schedule of busy professionals who plan conferences, workshops, and meetings, it is easy to engage in budgeting and leave only minimal time for strategic financial management. If this happens, it is important to modify your time management. Nothing should have a higher priority than allocating the time necessary to engage in strategic financial management.

Reasons for Engaging in Strategic Financial Management

Long-range financial health for an organization never happens by accident. Rather, it results from carefully and systematically developing specific strategies that, when combined, will ensure long-term financial security. Achieving this type of long-term success for an organization is one of the chief responsibilities of leaders. Few people in an organization will feel confident about the success and quality of programming if they are not assured of a leader's ability to manage a financially healthy operation. Without such professional credibility, it is difficult to provide the type of innovative, responsive leadership required in today's organizations that plan conferences, workshops, and meetings. There is fierce competition for business, and people who excel in both program development and strategic financial management are the most sought after for key leadership positions.

Therefore, one of the highest priorities for people who plan conferences, workshops, and meetings should be to become expert in strategic financial management as a basis for developing and enhancing their career. This expertise, in turn, will assist the employing organization to achieve excellence as well. Thus, there are important personal and organizational payoffs for becoming skilled in strategic financial management.

Another reason for leaders to become expert at strategic financial management is to fulfill their ethical obligation to the organization employing them. Today's complex, constantly changing organizations require leaders with a wide variety of skills. Not only must leaders be skilled at program development; they must also become skilled in such areas as human resource management, creating adaptive mechanisms to better serve our clients, and managing on a daily basis the change occurring within society. These skills form the foundation for expertise in strategic financial management. Leaders who become skilled in all of these areas can provide the best possible leadership for their organizations.

This type of leadership emphasizes constant organizational renewal. We are working with the best-educated work force in the history of humankind, and because of this high educational level, staff want to play a role in defining the future directions of their organizations. We can best help them do this by providing leadership that emphasizes the importance of the role that staff play in creating a learning organization — an organization that has created the type of processes, structures, and mechanisms that enable it to constantly learn about itself and thus to maintain a high degree of adaptability to its environment.

Characteristics of an Effective
Strategic Financial Management System

Successful strategic financial management occurs as a result of the interaction of many complex systems, procedures, processes, and other variables. First, the most successful strategic financial management systems provide for the creation of effective procedures for planning individual program budgets. For this to be achieved, everyone in charge of an individual program must learn the few basic accounting concepts presented in this book. They must use similar budget forms and planning processes in order to ensure consistency, and they must understand how administrative fee cost recovery to pay for staff time and other expenses is calculated in their organization. Developing this type of base-line data is critical to effective program and budget development. The remaining chapters in this book illustrate how to do this.

Second, it is important to establish clear responsibility for budget management. In most organizations, this is a straightforward procedure. The person in charge of planning the program is also in charge of planning and managing the budget. One of the most often-made mistakes in planning conferences, workshops, and meetings is failing to clearly establish exactly who is in charge of developing and managing the budget. Above all, never appoint cochairs, comanagers, or committees to manage a program budget. When this happens, no one ends up in charge, and as a result, no one is ultimately accountable for the success or failure of the budget planning and management process.

Third, it is important to design systems for effectively monitoring all income and expenses for individual programs. To achieve success in the budget management process for individual programs, program managers must be able to access reliable information regarding all income and expenditures. This information needs to be constantly updated so that it is accurate within the last twenty-four hours.

Fourth, flexibility in handling unforeseen problems must be planned for as an integral part of a budget. Between the time a budget is planned and the time a program takes place, there will inevitably be expenses that could not have been predicted. Therefore, it is important to always allocate some percentage of a budget to cover these unforeseen expenses. While the percentage for these miscellaneous expenses will vary from organization to organization, many professional planners of conferences, workshops, and meetings find that 10 percent of all identified expenses is adequate. If less than 10 percent is planned to cover miscellaneous expenses, there should be a justifiable reason for this lower figure. The budget forms shown in the illustrations in this book demonstrate how to plan for these miscellaneous expenses.

Fifth, it is important to achieve financial goals that have been established for individual program budgets as well as for an office as a whole. It is essential to take a conservative approach to budgeting and strategic financial management. For example, a common mistake is overestimating the number of people who will attend a program. Nothing guarantees failure in budgeting faster than this. It is important that organizations develop reliable historical data regarding average program attendance. Ultimately, the real issue becomes who pays for the losses if the required number of people to break even do not register for the program.

Sixth, implementing strategic financial management assists in developing a learning organization. Ensure that as part of overall planning you always analyze your successes and failures in the total financial management process. If your office is large enough so that you have several program planners, it is important to do this planning as a team. An effective strategy is to ask each team member, as part of regularly scheduled staff meetings, to present a comprehensive analysis of the successes and failures encountered in planning and managing individual program budgets. This helps to raise the consciousness of everyone in the group about strategic financial management. If you are a one-person office or simply someone who is charged with planning a program in connection with your other duties in an organization, you should also conduct this type of analysis after a program is over.

Seventh, it is important to learn from successes and failures and to change financial management procedures as appropriate. It is one thing to contemplate what you would do differently if you could repeat the program. It is another thing to keep an ongoing list of lessons you have learned so these ideas can be integrated into your daily budget planning and management. We often learn important lessons from listening to others analyze their successes and failures. Sometimes our own learning, especially from our failures, is so painful or embarrassing that we tend to avoid the analytical process that can reveal what might have been done differently. Maintaining an ongoing list of lessons learned assists in enhancing our skills for the future.

Ensuring that the above factors become a part of an effective strategic financial management system should be a priority for all staff members. It is through this constant analysis and attention to our own lifelong learning that we become skilled experts at budgeting and strategic financial management.

Assumptions Underlying
Strategic Financial Management

Planning for strategic financial management is like planning for the good management of other resources in the organization. It requires an effective set of assumptions that can be used to guide daily thinking and behavior. All our leadership initiatives or actions rest on a set of assumptions. Nothing is more powerful in the busy world of today's rapidly changing organizations than the leaders' assumptions or philosophical beliefs about people, time, money, and other resources.

Because assumptions are such powerful forces in guiding our daily behavior, it is important to develop a set of reliable, workable assumptions related to strategic financial management. These assumptions provide the beginning of a road map that enables leaders to develop the best possible strategies for financial management of the organization as a whole as well as individual programs.

The first important assumption underlying strategic financial management is that the process of planning and managing a successful budget involves more than just the mathematical calculation of the individual items in the budget. It also usually involves creative program planning, management of conflict about the allocation of scarce resources, and last-minute adjustments to ensure that the program content and finances work hand in hand to complement each other.

Another important assumption is that positive attitudes toward the budgeting process and the strategic financial management system do not occur by accident but are the result of a conscious choice by leaders to create and maintain them. Good budgeting is a complex process with many variables, some of which cannot be controlled by program planners. Therefore, language used to describe the process of managing money is very important. The language should be positive, it should deal with difficult issues, and it should become part of the shared vision of everyone in the office.

It is also important to build in a series of checks and balances to the budget management process to act as early warning signs in case budgets get into trouble. For example, establish clear guidelines for how often program planners should review and update the budget for an upcoming program. While these guidelines will vary widely from organization to organization, each organization should develop its own set of clearly understood procedures for accomplishing this type of regular review. As a rule of thumb, consider reviewing a budget at least every thirty days until the program is two months away. After this, it will probably be necessary to review the budget at least once a week. During the last thirty days before a program, it is often necessary to review a budget almost daily until the required number of registrations is secured to ensure that the program breaks even.

Building these types of checks and balances into the budget management process means that potential budget problems can be identified and addressed before they turn into a crisis. The assumptions outlined above are concrete enough to be converted into measurable events and activities. Until each of these assumptions is established, it is difficult to successfully implement a comprehensive system of strategic financial management.

Strategic financial management is not a passing fad. It should be a part of the foundation underlying almost every organizational decision. Strategic financial management is not a simple act that has a beginning and an end. Rather, it involves integrating sound fiscal planning processes into the daily fabric of organizational life. Therefore, attention to strategic financial management should be an important element of almost all daily decisions related to planning conferences, workshops, and meetings.

Strategic financial management is a method of allocating financial resources. It becomes the driving force for translating plans into action. It establishes accountability. It determines the cost effectiveness of the return on investment in programming. Thus, designing and implementing strategic financial management are among the most critical factors in ensuring the long-term health of an organization.

Four Rules for Success
in Strategic Financial Management

Most advice about strategic financial management can best be described as guidelines and principles that can be adapted to fit the specific needs of all organizations that plan conferences, workshops, and meetings. However, the following are four never-to-be-violated rules that form the foundation for becoming successful at strategic financial management:

1. Learn your budget.
2. Learn your budget.
3. Learn your budget.
4. Learn how to *manage* your budget.

The term *budget* is the generic term referring to the plan for income and expenses related to a specific program. Thus, a budget might be developed for a specific conference, workshop, or meeting. However, the term *budget* is also used as a collective noun that refers to a series of budgets. For example, a program planner in the training and development department of a large corporation might plan thirty individual training programs during a year with thirty different budgets. This program planner would refer to the *budget* for each separate program. However, this same program planner might be required to wrap up all thirty of these budgets into an overall budget.

It is essential to learn the many details of each budget under your control. In addition, it is important to learn how your budgets feed into the larger financial picture for the organization. One of the most common mistakes in the business of planning conferences, workshops, and meetings is assuming that more time needs to be devoted to program planning than to budget development and management. In reality, most programs require approximately equal time for both of these activities if they are to be successful.

It is one thing to learn about the mechanics of a budget or a series of budgets. It is another thing to learn how to effectively manage these budgets on a daily basis. Successful budget management involves learning how to manage the conflict that often occurs when resources are limited and expectations for enhanced programming are high. It involves building in a percentage to cover miscellaneous expenses that inevitably occur between the time a budget is planned and a program actually takes place. It often involves having to say no to requests for additional, last-minute resources when the number of registrations required to break even has not materialized.

It is only through daily dedication to developing specific strategies to effectively manage all the financial resources under a leader's control that overall strategic financial management is achieved.

Establishing Clear Goals: The Key to Successful Strategic Financial Management

Goals are broad, general statements that provide a direction or vision for an organization. Without clear goals, organizations cannot easily adapt to today's rapidly changing environment. Therefore, establishing clear goals for the strategic management of financial resources is an important activity. These goals should state clearly what the organization wants to achieve. For example, the following financial goals are appropriate for a wide variety of organizations planning conferences, workshops, and meetings:

1. To develop a uniform system for planning all program budgets—a system that can be easily understood and learned by all staff members
2. To plan and manage budgets so there will be no surprises at the end of the fiscal year
3. To develop a system for monitoring budget records that can easily be updated every twenty-four hours so an accurate account of all income and expenses can be maintained for individual program accounts
4. To break even at the end of each year according to the overall budget planned for an office

The advantage of having a clear statement of overall goals is that everyone in the organization can develop a common set of expectations about the management of financial resources. These expectations should be understood by all the key players. In fact, many organizations find it helpful to print up their overall financial goals and distribute them to everyone concerned with managing conferences, workshops, and meetings. The advantage of this is that each individual program budget, as well as overall budgets for an office, can be developed in relation to these goals.

Summary

Budgeting and strategic financial planning are both important to organizational success. They form a symbiotic relationship in which each complements the other. Organizations that remain financially healthy establish clear goals for financial management and make sure that all staff understand these goals. All decisions that affect finances should be made with these goals in mind.

An important leadership skill in organizations that plan conferences, workshops, and meetings is the ability to achieve success with budgeting and strategic financial planning simultaneously. When this happens, daily decision making is enhanced, the foundation for long-range financial health is established, and expectations for personal as well as organizational success are clearly understood. This provides the foundation for providing leadership in creating a learning organization that is capable of adapting to the constantly changing demands of society.

2.

Creating a Budget
for One Program

Follow these five easy steps when creating a budget.

Planning a budget for a conference, workshop, or meeting is a very complex activity that requires attention to detail. This chapter identifies and analyzes the five steps to follow to create a budget for a single program. Mastering these five steps is essential to implementing comprehensive strategic financial management. No matter what size the program is, these five steps always remain the same.

Step 1: Accurately identify all expenses associated with a program.

Step 2: Clearly distinguish between fixed and variable expenses.

Step 3: Determine how many people can be expected to attend so that a break-even point can be established.

Step 4: Establish a registration fee that equals or exceeds the total expenses incurred for each registrant.

Step 5: Display budget data so that the logic of how the registration fee was established can be easily understood.

Case Study: Implementing the Five Steps

In this section, we consider each of these steps in detail through the use of a case study illustrating good budget planning principles. We then analyze the case study according to the five major steps in the budget planning process. This case illustrates how to plan a budget for a small, one-day program. However, the principles and guidelines discussed apply to small as well as large programs. The only difference in the budget planning process for a large program is that the budget form will be longer, with more spaces for identifying additional expenditures.

Kelly Tuffs is a program director in the Office of Executive Development in the College of Business Administration of a medium-size college. Kelly is in charge of working with the Department of Management to plan the budget for a one-day workshop entitled How to Plan and Run Effective Meetings.

Kelly needs to present the budget to a departmental planning committee composed of faculty members who are experts in the content area but have not had much experience at planning budgets for workshops. It is Kelly's job as program director to establish a registration fee that will break even with a modest number of people. Kelly knows that about a hundred people usually register for such workshops; therefore, Kelly reduces this average number of attendance by 25 percent and conservatively estimates seventy-five registrants to break even. Kelly knows from experience that rarely less than seventy-five people register for workshops sponsored by the Office of Executive Development.

Now Kelly needs to display the budget data in a written form so that people who have not had much experience at budgeting for workshops can easily understand how the registration fee was established. This form will include accurate projections of all program expenses: food, printing of brochures, mailing costs, and all other expenses associated with the program.

In addition to creating a break-even budget, Kelly and the committee are concerned about the quality of the program's content. Therefore, budgeting and program development become an integral part of the same process. One of the professors in the department states the issue this way: "We don't want a gimmicky presentation that emphasizes only superficial issues related to meeting management. We want to offer a program that will actually help people. Becoming better at meeting management is a complex activity that spills over into all aspects of one's life. Therefore, we want to emphasize substantive content that concludes with practical suggestions and techniques that people can begin implementing immediately back home on their jobs."

In developing the overall plan for the workshop, Kelly follows the five steps previously listed. The remainder of this section illustrates how Kelly implements each of these five steps.

Step 1: Identify Expenses

The following list contains the best estimates for expenses in connection with Kelly's workshop. All these expenses are estimated according to reliable data. For example, before estimating costs for a program, Kelly will get a written contract guaranteeing prices for space and food from the hotel where the workshop will be held.

1. There will be only one program presenter for the entire day. Her name is Mary Winthrop, and her honorarium will be $2,000.
2. Kelly will pay $500 travel expenses for the speaker and $175 to cover other expenses, such as food, hotel room, and transportation to and from the airport.
3. Lunch will be served at the workshop. The cost will be $12 per person.
4. Kelly will print 10,000 brochures at a cost of twenty cents each.
5. There will be a refreshment break in the morning and another in the afternoon. Each break will cost $2 per person.

6.   Kelly will pick up the cost of coffee served during two plan-
     ning committee meetings as part of the program budget.
     This will total $17.86.
7.   Each attendee will receive a registration packet contain-
     ing a name badge, a pencil, paper, a roster of attendees,
     and other information. This registration packet will cost
     $5 per attendee to assemble.
8.   The Department of Management has requested three com-
     plimentary registrations for graduate students. The cost
     of these is figured as three times the total variable costs per
     person.
9.   Graphic design for the brochure will cost $300.
10. Typesetting the brochure will cost $175.
11. Kelly needs to charge an $8,000 administrative fee to help
     cover the costs of running the Office of Executive Devel-
     opment. This will pay for general office overhead expenses
     that cannot easily be assigned to any specific program.
12. General duplicating of materials related to the workshop
     is estimated to cost $265.
13. It will cost twenty-one cents each for bulk-rate mailing of
     10,000 brochures advertising the program.
14. Additional advertising will cost $300.
15. As a contingency factor, Kelly plans to include 10 per-
     cent of the total costs per person to cover miscellaneous
     expenses that are likely to occur as the program planning
     proceeds.
16. Since registrants are allowed to register by credit card,
     4.5 percent of the total per person registration fee must
     be included to pay the bank the credit card processing fee.
17. A 15 percent gratuity will be added to the total bill for
     all food before tax is charged.
18. A 6 percent state sales tax will be added to the food total
     after the gratuity has been charged.
19. It will cost $675 to rent mailing lists from various mailing
     list houses.

   These are the major expenses that Kelly identifies as necessary for a successful program. Since it is important to always
plan for a contingency fund to cover expenses that inevitably

will arise between the time the budget is set and the time the program actually takes place, Kelly has allowed 10 percent of the fixed costs to cover this. This is an important item to build into any budget. As a rule of thumb, 10 percent of any program budget should be allocated as a contingency fund. After examining your own historical data, you may find that you need to add more than this amount for individual programs.

Step 2: Distinguish Between Fixed and Variable Expenses

It is impossible to arrive at an accurate break-even figure to establish a registration fee without first clearly distinguishing between fixed and variable expenses. Fixed expenses consist of all expenses that will remain constant no matter how many people attend the workshop. For example, the cost of printing and mailing brochures to advertise the program is always a fixed expense. No matter how many people attend, this expense will have been incurred far in advance of the event and will not change. Other typical fixed expenses include graphic design for brochures, advertising, typesetting, and expenses associated with planning committees. Variable expenses are expenses that will vary depending on how many people attend the program. For example, if lunch costs $12 and twenty-five people attend, the total expenses for lunch will be $300; if fifty people register, the total cost will be $600.

An easy way to distinguish between fixed and variable expenses is to clearly separate these items on a list. Exhibit 2.1 shows how to do this for expenses identified by Kelly. Note that the 10 percent for miscellaneous expenses has not yet been figured. Nor has the 4.5 percent for the credit card fee been included. These expenses are figured in the next step.

Step 3: Determine a Break-Even Point

The following steps illustrate how a break-even point for expenses is determined.

1. Conservatively estimate how many people will register. Kelly estimates that seventy-five will attend.

Exhibit 2.1. Fixed and Variable Expenses.

Fixed expenses

Item number	Description	Amount
1.	Honorarium for Mary Winthrop	$2,000.00
2.	Travel and other expenses for speaker	675.00
4.	Printing of 10,000 brochures at $.20 each	2,000.00
6.	Coffee served to planning committee	17.86
8.	Three complimentary registrations (this is the sum of the per-person variable expenses times 3 people @ $24.50 each)	73.50
9.	Graphic design for brochure	300.00
10.	Typesetting for brochure	175.00
11.	Administrative fee	8,000.00
12.	General duplicating of materials	265.00
13.	Mailing of 10,000 brochures at $.21 each	2,100.00
14.	Additional advertising	300.00
19.	Rental of mailing lists	675.00
	Subtotal	$16,581,36

Per person variable expenses

Item number	Description	Amount
3.	Lunch	$12.00
5.	Two refreshment breaks at $2 each	4.00
7.	Registration packet	5.00
17.	Fifteen percent gratuity on the subtotal of all food before the sales tax is added	2.40
18.	Six percent state sales tax added to the food and gratuity subtotal of $18.40 per person	1.10
	Subtotal	$24.50

2. Divide the total fixed expenses of $16,581.36 by seventy-five. This provides the per person fixed expenses of $221.08.

3. Add to this the per person variable expenses of $24.50, for a per person subtotal of $245.58.

4. Add 10 percent to the subtotal of $245.58 to create a contingency fund to cover miscellaneous expenses. This brings the subtotal to $270.13.

5. Add 4.5 percent to cover the credit card processing fee. At $12.15 per person, this brings the total expenses per person to $282.29.

Later in the chapter, we show where to enter these dollar amounts on the budget form.

Step 4: Establish a Registration Fee That Is Equal to the Total Expenses Incurred for Each Registrant

The total expenses per person are $282.29. This figure is rounded up to the next five-dollar increment to establish a registration fee of $285. Do not under any circumstances round down the registration fee. For example, it is inappropriate to establish a registration fee of $270 for this program, because this will not cover all the projected expenses. If you wish to establish a lower registration fee, it will be necessary to create another version of the budget in which you eliminate enough expenses to make the total costs equal $270 per person with seventy-five registrants. Another way to lower the registration fee is to increase the number of people required to break even. However, there is a danger in doing this. It is entirely possible that you will increase the break-even number of registrations to a number higher than can reasonably be expected. When this happens, the question becomes who will pay for any possible losses.

It is equally important not to establish a registration fee greater than the actual expenses per person rounded up to the nearest five dollars. For example, in Kelly's case, it would be inappropriate to establish a registration fee of $350 with seventy-five people listed to break even. If you think the market will bear the $350 registration fee, then the number of people to break even must be refigured. This would lower the break-even figure to below seventy-five.

Step 5: Create an Easily Understood Budget Form

A budget should always be displayed in such a way that everyone can easily understand how the registration fee was established. The budget form in Exhibit 2.2 shows how to do this. Note that each expense item is clearly identified. Fixed expenses are listed on one side of the page and per person variable expenses on the other side. There is a clear internal logic to the budget form that leads the reader through the process of calculating a registration fee. The provision for miscellaneous expenditures is shown as an exact dollar amount. This is calculated as 10 percent of the subtotal of $245.58, or $24.55 per person.

There is also a provision for registrants paying by credit card. This is calculated as 4.5 percent of the subtotal of $270.13, or $12.15 per person. When providing the option of paying the registration fee by credit card, it is important to assume that everyone will choose this option when figuring the budget. While this will probably not happen, if it does and you have not provided for it, you will lose money.

The budget form is easy to program on an electronic spreadsheet using one of the popular personal computer software packages such as Excel or Lotus 1–2–3. Maintaining budget forms on electronic spreadsheets makes it easy to change any item and quickly get a printout showing how this change will affect the amount of the registration fee.

The sample budget form in Exhibit 2.2 is a prototype that can easily be modified for planning any type of conference, workshop, or meeting, no matter what the size. However, in modifying the form, it is important to do the following:

- Calculate fringe benefits for honoraria if this is a requirement of the organization. In our study here, fringe benefits do not have to be paid, since the presenter is not an employee of the sponsoring organization.
- List the most often used categories of expenses incurred in connection with a wide variety of conferences, workshops, and meetings. Blanks can easily be inserted for other expenses that might be required for a specific program. Additional expense items should be grouped according to large categories of expense types similar to the ones on the form in Exhibit 2.2 when you modify it to fit your individual needs.
- Plan a minimum of 10 percent of any budget to cover miscellaneous expenses.
- Calculate the cost for credit card registrations.

Exhibit 2.2. Sample Budget Form.

Fixed expenses		**Per person variable expenses**		
Presenters				
Honorarium—Mary Winthrop	$2,000.00	Registration packet	$5.00	
Fringe benefits		Food		
Travel	675.00	Lunch @ $12		
		Two breaks @ $4		
Advertising		Food subtotal $16		
Printing 10,000 brochures @ $.20	2,000.00	Gratuity @ 15%		
Graphic design	300.00	of $16 = $2.40		
Typesetting	175.00	Total food	18.40	
Mailing 10,000 brochures @ $.21	2,100.00	6% sales tax on		
Additional ads	300.00	$18.40 food	1.10	
Mailing list rental	675.00			
		Total per person		
Administrative		**variable expenses**	$24.50	
Administrative fee	8,000.00			
Materials/supplies				
Duplicating	265.00			
General expenses				
Coffee	17.86			
Three complimentary registrations				
@ $24.50 each	73.50			
Subtotal fixed expenses	$16,581.36			
Divided by 75 people				
to break even	221.08			
Add total per person				
variable expenses	24.50			
Subtotal	$245.58			
Add 10% miscellaneous	24.55			
Subtotal	$270.13			
Add 4.5% credit card fee	12.15			
Total expenses per person	282.29	**Registration fee per person**		$285

- Clearly distinguish between fixed and variable costs.
- Provide for covering the costs of complimentary registrations. Remember, there is no such thing as a free registration. Complimentary guests eat the same lunch, partake of the same refreshment breaks, and receive the same registration packet. The cost of complimentary registrations must always be figured as the total of all direct variable expenses times the number of complimentary registrations, then converted to a fixed expense item as shown on the budget form in Exhibit 2.2.

Successful Budget Planning

Successful budget planning is not a magical or mystical process. Mostly it consists of hard work, skillful negotiation, revisions, compromise, and coming to terms with what one can afford in relation to what the public is willing to pay. The following guidelines should be carefully followed in the planning of budgets.

Allow everyone involved with planning a program access to the budget. This will usually produce a better budget as well as higher satisfaction with it. Budgeting should never be a secret process. Involve the necessary key stakeholders in planning, analysis, and discussion.

Early in the program development process, introduce a tentative rough draft of the budget. This is especially important if others, such as planning and advisory groups, must approve the budget, because this will help them to come to terms with what is often a large gap between the initial wish list and what is realistic to include given practical financial constraints.

Acknowledge that it often takes five to eight drafts before a program budget meets the goals of the program and the sponsoring organization. Revising budgets and producing additional rough drafts are a natural part of the planning process.

Accept the fact that constant negotiation is an integral part of the budget planning process. Many of us have visions of program content and excellence that far exceed our resources. Therefore, it is not unusual for individuals and planning committees to initially concentrate only on program content, with little regard for the actual expenses involved. An effective way to bring people back to reality during the program development process is to create a budget for the grand vision that people initially consider. When they see how this grand vision affects the per person registration fee, they will often quickly insist on instituting an expense reduction process geared to the realities of what people will pay to attend a specific program.

Acknowledge that the negotiation process often produces conflict that must be managed. Reducing expenses for programs can often produce conflict during planning sessions. People argue for their point of view regarding content, method of presentation, and marketing plans. The conflict that is produced as a result of these discussions, debates, and analysis is a natural and inevitable part of the program planning process. Therefore, plan for managing conflict for productive results rather than trying to eliminate it.

Leaders who follow these basic hints will establish a firm base for developing creative budgeting strategies appropriate to their own individual programs. Such leaders see negotiation, compromise, and conflict management as a natural part of their daily activity.

Summary

Budget planning is a highly complex and time-consuming activity. However, it is also a highly creative act, because it often requires skill in working through conflict, a knowledge of program development principles, marketing expertise, and experience with programming spreadsheets on personal computers. Budget forms can be individualized to fit the needs of organizations and specific programs. However, no matter what size the program, the five basic steps for budget planning presented in this chapter remain the same.

3.

The Importance of Recovering Administrative Overhead

Carefully planning for administrative expense cost recovery is an important aspect of strategic financial management.

Most organizations that plan conferences, workshops, and meetings for which a registration fee is charged must recover either a portion or all of their general overhead expenses. Overhead consists of those expenses that cannot be easily attributed to a specific program. For example, in an office such as the one discussed in Chapter Two, it usually is not possible to assign a staff member to plan just one program for an entire year. Therefore, the time that staff members spend planning and administering programs must be prorated to all the programs they coordinate. This can easily be accomplished by charging an administrative fee to each program's budget to recover these costs.

Identifying General Office Overhead Expenses

An example of general office overhead is the use of office equipment. While office equipment is used in connection with all programs, it is usually not practical to prorate its use to individual programs. Therefore, this use is classified as a general office expense or overhead cost. (The terms *general office expenses* and *overhead* are used interchangeably in this chapter.) Typical categories of general office expenses or overhead for a department that plans conferences, workshops, and meetings as part of its total work load include staff salaries and fringe benefits, office supplies, office equipment, telephones, professional development travel, utilities, custodial services, and capital improvements. Some of these expenses may actually be chargeable to specific programs. For example, travel related to an individual program should be charged to that program. However, general administrative travel or staff travel to professional development activities, would be included as part of general office expenses.

Categories of general expenses will vary from organization to organization, but one fact usually remains constant: all or at least a significant portion of overhead expenses will usually be prorated to individual programs for cost recovery. There are five basic issues to consider when developing a cost recovery system through charging administrative fees to individual programs.

First, it is important to create a comprehensive office budget in which all general office expenses are estimated for an entire year. You often will hear people in charge of planning conferences, workshops, and meetings ask, "What percentage of my expenses should I charge for overhead?" The answer is that it all depends on what your general office budget is for a year and what portion of these expenses your employing organization expects you to recover. Without developing a budget for all general office overhead, it is impossible to determine what percentage should be charged to individual programs. In fact, one of the most often-made mistakes is establishing a percentage of revenue to allocate to administrative fee cost recovery without knowing specifically what total dollar amount is needed each year to cover general office expenses. This chapter explains how to develop a general office overhead budget. Subsequent chapters show how to charge general overhead expenses back to individual programs through an administrative fee.

Second, if you are required to recover all or a portion of your general overhead expenses, it is important to develop strategies for planning a total yearly schedule of events. Until you have developed a schedule of the total programs for a year, it is impossible to calculate what administrative fee you need to charge individual programs. Thus, engaging in yearly strategic planning is essential to financial success in the business of conferences, workshops, and meetings.

Third, it is important to create a reliable, easy-to-use accounting system for monitoring the income and expense budget for the entire office. This accounting system must be updated every few days to provide an accurate account of the office's finances. Posting all income and expenses to every account every day is most desirable. A common mistake is not creating an accounting system that will provide for this type of constant updating. When such constant updating is not done, it is too easy to overspend budgets. In addition, the constant updating provides a check-and-balance procedure in which early warning systems can identify problems with the budget as it plays itself out during the course of a year. These red flags, or early warning systems, are essential to overall successful financial planning.

Fourth, it is important to conduct a comprehensive budget review of each program, including the general overhead budget, every thirty days. Doing this enables you to develop systems for increasing income and/or reducing expenses if data suggest that the office will not break even as a total budget entity. This system should provide for laying out, on a series of electronic spreadsheets, a comprehensive listing of all programs at the beginning of each new fiscal year. When the income and expenses for these programs and the budget for general office expenses are balanced, you are ready to implement the budget for a fiscal year. Illustrations throughout the remainder of the book show how to do this.

Fifth, it is important to allow all staff access to the office budget so that they can understand its component parts. This will enable everyone to comprehend why administrative fees are established. It will also enable staff to understand why it is so important to constantly monitor the status of all administrative fee cost recovery for the entire office. Nothing will ensure financial failure faster than approaching budget planning as if the process required secrecy.

The remainder of this chapter illustrates how to create a budget in which all general office expenses are estimated for an entire fiscal year. Subsequent chapters address the remaining steps required to achieve a total comprehensive cost recovery system.

Case Study: Estimating
General Office Expenses for a Fiscal Year

This case study continues the scenario of Kelly Tuffs, introduced in Chapter One. This case and the accompanying exhibits show how to display the expense portion of an office budget for a fiscal year.

The Office of Executive Development has eleven employees, including Kelly. Each year, Kelly plans a budget for the upcoming fiscal year that contains projections for both income and expenses. The expense side of the budget for general office expenses is shown in Exhibit 3.1.

These expenses are divided into two broad categories—personnel and general office expenses. Salaries for all office personnel are listed on a line-item basis on the spreadsheet. Fringe benefits are added because they are part of direct expenses. Next, general office expenses are listed. This list can be as broad or as specific as necessary. In Exhibit 3.1., broad categories of expense items are listed.

In addition to specific expense categories, the budget includes a 10 percent allocation for miscellaneous expenses. This is designed to cover all the unplanned-for expenses that inevitably arise between the time a budget is planned at the beginning of a fiscal year and the time it is closed out at the end of the fiscal year. Whatever guidelines and regulations govern your budget preparation and accounting system, it is important to plan for unexpected expenses. If this is not done, the office will have no contingency fund to cover unanticipated expenses that inevitably occur during the course of a year. It should be noted,

Exhibit 3.1. Projected General Office Expenses for a Fiscal Year.

Personal expenses		Amount	Subtotals	
Tuffs		$60,000		
Smithson		30,500		
Johnson		31,000		
Timoreaux		35,200		
Walters		26,000		
Matthews		15,725		
Landon		16,875		
Lester		16,847		
Wextler		24,857		
Letterman		22,900		
Weston		19,087		
	Subtotal		$298,991	
Fringes @ 25%			74,748	
General office expenses				← Note: None of these general office expenses can be directly attributed to any specific program. Specific program expenses are always charged to the appropriate program.
Printing and duplicating		10,000		
General postage		5,000		
Phones		12,750		
Office equipment		22,500		
General travel		12,500		
General supplies		22,000		
Custodial services		17,780		
	Subtotal		$102,530	
Total salaries, fringes, and general office expenses			$476,269	
Plus 10% miscellaneous			47,627	
	Grand total		**$523,896**	

however, that many local, state, and federal governmental agencies will not allow for any budget line-item category labeled as miscellaneous. If this is the case, leaders often build their miscellaneous category into other line items by increasing these expense projections.

Exhibit 3.2 shows a more detailed budget using the same data presented in Exhibit 3.1. In Exhibit 3.2, the large general budget categories under office expenses are subdivided even further. This more detailed budget breakdown can force the office to show on paper what specific dollar amounts in each broad budget category are allocated to specific expenditures, which encourages people to be more specific in planning a year in advance for their expenditures. It can also highlight potential savings that can be achieved as the year proceeds if income does not meet expectations. For example, the expenditure of $2,000 for a new desk and chair shown in Exhibit 3.2 might be deferred until the end of the year, when a more reliable estimate of income to offset general office expenses is available. If at that time the general overhead budget is projected to break even with the expenditure, the purchase could be made.

The bottom line in Exhibit 3.2 is that the office estimates it will spend $523,896 during the next fiscal year. Until this type of bottom-line budget estimating of all general office expenses has been established, there is no way to develop a reliable system for charging back administrative fees to individual programs. We now know that Kelly's office must plan to recover a total of $523,896 in administrative fees and other revenues from programs for the coming fiscal year. Chapter Four explains how to do this through an administrative fee charge-back system.

Practical Tips for
Developing the General Overhead Budget

When developing a general overhead budget, there is often a tendency to rush through the process and put down figures in order to finish this project quickly. However, it is important to devote as much time and attention to developing a general overhead budget as you devote to planning a budget for a large, complicated conference, workshop, or meeting.

Exhibit 3.2. Detailed General Office Expenses.

		Amount	Subtotals
Personnel expenses			
Tuffs		$60,000	
Smithson		30,500	
Johnson		31,000	
Timoreaux		35,200	
Walters		26,000	
Matthews		15,725	
Landon		16,875	
Lester		16,847	
Wextler		24,857	
Letterman		22,900	
Weston		19,087	
	Subtotal		$298,991
Fringes @ 25%			74,748
General office expenses			10,000
Printing and duplicating			
Copy machine	$7,000		
Paper	1,500		
Mechanicals	500		
General office brochures	500		
Typesetting	250		
Graphic design	250		
General postage			5,000
Bulk mailings — general	3,000		
First-class mail	2,000		
Phones			12,750
Monthly charges	6,850		
Five new phones	500		
Monthly long distance	5,400		
Office equipment			
Five personal computers	18,050		22,500
Refills for laser printers	1,000		
One desk-top calculator	450		

Exhibit 3.2. Detailed General Office Expenses, Cont'd.

New desk and chair	2,000		
Display racks	1,000		
General travel			
Professional development	6,000		12,500
Administrative	6,500		
General supplies			22,000
Paper	4,500		
Miscellaneous supplies	8,400		
Cleaning materials	8,400		
New vacuum cleaner	700		
Custodial services			17,780
Cleaning contract	17,780		
Total salaries, fringes, and general office expenses			$476,269
Plus 10% miscellaneous			47,627
		Grand total	$523,896

Historical data can be very beneficial in developing a general overhead budget. If accurate expense records have been kept in the past, they can provide an excellent basis for estimating expenses in each of the line-item categories. If such have not been kept, then it is important to institute such a record-keeping procedure immediately to serve as a planning tool for the future. In addition, once dollar amounts have been estimated for each of the line items, it is important to establish a monthly accounting procedure that will provide a check and balance against overspending in any category. The best way to achieve this is by establishing a comprehensive budget review for all general expense categories every thirty days so that expenses in all categories can be carefully monitored and overspending avoided.

Finally, the office should decide exactly who is in charge of planning and monitoring the general office overhead budget. In most cases, the director or head of the office should be charged with this responsibility and should not delegate it to anyone else. Others can assist with record keeping, but responsibility for the ultimate success or failure of the budget should be vested in the director, who should work closely with all staff to plan for success in this area.

Summary

An office that only occasionally plans a conference, workshop, or meeting may not be required to recover any of its overhead costs. Often such overhead costs are simply viewed by the organization as in-kind contributions. For example, a university history department may plan one conference every two years for a professional association of historians. If the program is small, a departmental secretary may handle the registration process as well as a number of other administrative details. The professors themselves may contribute their time to the planning process. In this case, a general office budget overhead would not be necessary.

However, if an office plans a number of conferences, workshops, and meetings and the parent organization does not provide for absorbing all expenses for general office overhead, including personnel as well as operating expenses, then a general office overhead budget will need to be developed before it will be possible to determine how to recover expenses through charging an administrative fee to individual programs.

Offices that are usually expected to recover all or part of general overhead expenses include training and development departments in some business, industry, and governmental organizations; training departments in hospitals and other types of health care agencies; conference offices in colleges and universities; education departments in museums; and offices that plan short-term workshops for leisure activities.

When a general office overhead budget similar to the one shown in Exhibit 3.1 has been laid out, it is possible to determine how to assess administrative fees to individual programs. The next chapter shows how to do this.

4.

How to Recover
Administrative Overhead

There are four basic ways to recover enough
money to pay for administrative overhead.

Exhibit 3.1 in Chapter Three shows that the Office of Executive
Development estimates its general operating expenses for the
year to be $523,896. With this knowledge, Kelly Tuffs, the di-
rector of that office, can begin creating alternative ways to develop a comprehensive system for charging back administrative
fees to individual programs. These administrative fees, plus any
additional positive balance for all programs, must equal $523,896
for the budget to balance.

Kelly begins this planning process by creating the following rough calculations. The office has scheduled fifty programs
for the year. The figure of $523,896 divided by fifty programs
equals $10,477.92 as an average administrative fee charge-back
for every program. The first rough calculation provides Kelly
with valuable information. Kelly knows that some of the planned

programs will not possibly recover $10,477 each. However, Kelly also knows that the office has planned three large programs that are projected to recover more than this. Therefore, Kelly develops another rough calculation.

By carefully examining the individual budgets for each of these three large programs, Kelly determines that each should net $50,000 through administrative fee charge-backs. This will total $150,000 to apply toward covering the administrative overhead. Therefore, Kelly reduces the $523,896 that must be made in administrative charge-backs by $150,000, leaving $373,896 to be recovered through the remaining forty-seven programs. He quickly calculates that $373,896 divided by forty-seven equals $7,955.23 that needs to be recovered by each of the remaining programs. Rounding off this figure, Kelly determines that it is necessary to recover an average of $8,000 in administrative fees for each program.

Using these very rough calculations, Kelly is now able to begin the process of deciding how best to charge back administrative fees to individual programs.

Four Methods for Administrative Fee Cost Recovery

Professionals who plan a wide variety of conferences, workshops, and meetings have found that there are four basic ways to recover administrative overhead through charging back administrative fees to individual programs (Wagner, 1981; Simerly, 1990a).

Flat Administrative Fee

With this method, a fixed dollar amount is recovered in the form of an administrative fee. Exhibit 4.1 shows a budget form in which a flat administrative fee is charged as a fixed expense to a program. In this budget, an administrative fee of $8,000 is recovered as a flat fee. This is a relatively easy method of administrative fee cost recovery because it is so simple. You simply decide on an appropriate flat fee. However, it is important to keep in mind when determining the amount of the flat fee that this must be done in relation to the entire general overhead expenses for a year.

Exhibit 4.1. Flat Administrative Fee Cost Recovery.

Fixed expenses		Per person variable expenses	
Presenters			
Honorarium — Mary Winthrop	$2,000.00	Registration packet	$5.00
Fringe benefits		Food	
Travel	675.00	Lunch @ $12	
		Two breaks @ $4	
Advertising		Food subtotal $16	
Printing 10,000 brochures @ $.20	2,000.00	Gratuity @ 15%	
Graphic design	300.00	of $16 = $2.40	
Typesetting	175.00	Total food	18.40
Mailing 10,000 brochures @ $.21	2,100.00	6% sales tax on	
Additional ads	300.00	$18.40 food	1.10
Mailing list rental	675.00		
		Total per person	
Administrative		variable expenses	$24.50
Administrative fee	8,000.00	←Note that $8,000	
		has been charged as a fixed	
Materials/supplies		administrative fee.	
Duplicating	265.00		
General expenses			
Coffee	17.86		
Three complimentary registrations			
@ $24.50 each	73.50		
Subtotal fixed expenses	$16,581.36		
Divided by 75 people			
to break even	221.08		
Add total per person			
variable expenses	24.50		
		Total administrative	
Subtotal	$245.58	fee cost recovery	
		Fixed fee	$8,000
Add 10% miscellaneous	24.55		
Subtotal	$270.13		
Add 4.5% credit card fee	12.15		
Total expenses per person	$ 282.29	Registration fee per person	$285

For example, since Kelly needs to recover a total of $523,896, if each program recovered a flat administrative fee of only $2,000, the office would need to conduct 262 programs to recover enough money to pay for general office overhead ($523,896 in total office overhead divided by $2,000 for each administrative fee equals 261.94, or 262 programs to break even). This may or may not be achievable, depending on plans for a total year's schedule of programs.

Per Person Variable Fee

This method establishes a per person dollar amount of the registration fee to be recovered for overhead. This amount is listed under variable expenses as shown in Exhibit 4.2. An analysis of Exhibit 4.2 shows that the administrative fee has been moved from the fixed expense column on the left of the budget form to the variable expense column on the right. A $107 per person variable fee is charged to recover administrative expenses. Thus, $107 times seventy-five people to break even would yield an administrative cost recovery of $8,025.

Note that in Exhibit 4.2, the expenses for the complimentary registrations are not recalculated from Exhibit 4.1. The reason for this is that each of the three complimentary registrants will actually consume the items subtotaled in the amount of $24.50 in Exhibit 4.2. Because these registrants do not contribute to the administrative fee cost recovery of $107 per person, they become a part of direct, fixed expenses.

Percentage of Total Expenses

Sometimes the most appropriate method for administrative fee cost recovery is the method that calculates the fee as a percentage of the total expenses for the entire program. Exhibit 4.3 shows a budget form that illustrates how to do this. Using this method, a 76 percent administrative fee is added to the subtotal of $159.68 of all expenses. This 76 percent equals $121.35; multiplied by seventy-five anticipated registrants, this yields a total administrative fee cost recovery of $9,101.25. This amount

Exhibit 4.2. Per Person Variable Fee Cost Recovery.

Fixed expenses		Per person variable expenses	
Presenters			
Honorarium — Mary Winthrop	$2,000.00	Registration packet	$5.00
Fringe benefits		Food	
Travel	675.00	Lunch @ $12	
		Two breaks @ $4	
Advertising		Food subtotal $16	
Printing 10,000 brochures @ $.20	2,000.00	Gratuity @ 15%	
Graphic design	300.00	of $16 = $2.40	
Typesetting	175.00	Total food	18.40
Mailing 10,000 brochures @ $.21	2,100.00	6% sales tax on	
Additional ads	300.00	$18.40 food	1.10
Mailing list rental	675.00		
		Subtotal	$24.50
Administrative			
Administrative fee			
		Administrative fee	107.00
Materials/supplies			
Duplicating	265.00	Note the addition of the $107 per person administrative fee. The $2,000 fixed administrative fee has been eliminated.	
General expenses			
Coffee	17.86		
Three complimentary registrations			
@ $24.50 each	73.50		
Subtotal fixed expenses	$8,581.36	**Total per person**	
Divided by 75 people		**Variable expenses**	$131.50
to break even	114.41		
Add total per person		**Total administrative fee cost recovery**	
variable expenses	131.50	Fixed fee 0.00	
Subtotal	$245.91	Per person variable fee 8,025.00 (75 × $107)	
Add 10% miscellaneous	24.59	**Total** $8,025.00	
Subtotal	$270.50		
Add 4.5% credit card fee	12.17		
Total expenses per person	$ 282.67	**Registration fee**	$285.00

Exhibit 4.3. Percentage of Total Expenses Cost Recovery.

Fixed expenses		Per person variable expenses	
Presenters			
Honorarium—Mary Winthrop	$2,000.00	Registration packet	$ 5.00
Fringe benefits		Food	
Travel	675.00	Lunch @ $12	
		Two breaks @ $4	
Advertising		Food subtotal $16	
Printing 10,000 brochures @ $.20	2,000.00	Gratuity @ 15%	
Graphic design	300.00	of $16 = $2.40	
Typesetting	175.00	Total food	18.40
Mailing 10,000 brochures @ $.21	2,100.00	6% sales tax on	
Additional ads	300.00	$18.40 food	1.10
Mailing list rental	675.00		
		Total per person	
Materials/supplies		**variable expenses**	$24.50
Duplicating	265.00		
		Per person administrative fee	
Administrative			
Administrative fee			
General expenses		Note that both the flat fee and the per person variable fee for administrative cost recovery have been removed.	
Coffee	17.86		
Three complimentary registrations			
@ $24.50 each	73.50		
Subtotal fixed expenses	$8,581.36		
Divided by 75 people			
to break even	114.41		
Add total per person			
variable expenses	24.50		
Subtotal	$138.91		
Add 10% miscellaneous	13.89		
Subtotal	$152.80		
Add 4.5% credit card fee	6.88		
		Note that administrative costs are recovered through a 76% administrative fee.	
Subtotal expenses per person	$159.68		
76% administrative fee	121.35		

Exhibit 4.3. Percentage of Total Expenses Cost Recovery, Cont'd.

Total expenses	$281.03	Total administrative fee cost recovery (75 people × $121.35 = $9,101.25)		
per person				
		Registration fee	$285.00	

can be increased or decreased by changing the percentage allocated to the total expenses for the administrative fee cost recovery. However, it is important to note that the program must recover a minimum of $8,000 that Kelly needs to contribute to general overhead expenses.

The Combination Method

Many organizations use a combination of methods to recover general overhead expenses. The budget in Exhibit 4.4 shows how to do this. This budget form uses a combination of the administrative fee cost recovery methods discussed above. Thus, the total program budget recovers the following amounts:

Fixed Fee— $1,000.00
$1,000 is charged as a fixed fee.

Per Person Variable Fee $5,625.00
A per person variable fee of $75 is
charged resulting in a total of $5,625
(calculated as $75 times 75 people).

Percentage of Total Expenses $4,309.50
22% of $261.21 = $57.46 × 75 people

Total $10,934.50

Thus, a total of $10,934.50 in administrative fees will be recovered.

Exhibit 4.4. Combination Method Cost Recovery.

Fixed expenses		Per person variable expenses	
Presenters			
Honorarium—Mary Winthrop	$2,000.00	Registration packet	$ 5.00
Fringe benefits		Food	
Travel	675.00	Lunch @ $12	
		Two breaks @ $4	
Advertising		Food subtotal $16	
Printing 10,000 brochures @ $.20	2,000.00	Gratuity @ 15%	
Graphic design	300.00	of $16 = $2.40	
Typesetting	175.00	Total food	18.40
Mailing 10,000 brochures @ $.21	2,100.00	6% sales tax on	
Additional ads	300.00	$18.40 food	1.10
Mailing list rental	675.00		
		Subtotal	$24.50
Materials/supplies			
Duplicating	265.00	Administrative fee	75.00
Administrative		A combination of methods is used to recover administrative fees.	
Administrative fee	1,000.00		
General expenses			
Coffee	17.86		
Three complimentary registrations @ $24.50 each	73.50		
		Total per person	
Subtotal fixed expenses	$9,581.36	**variable expenses**	**$99.50**
Divided by 75 people			
to break even	127.75	**Total administrative fee cost recovery**	
Add total per person		Fixed fee $1,000	
variable expenses	99.50	Per person variable fee $5,625.00 ($75 × 75 people)	
Subtotal	$227.25	Percentage of fixed expenses $4,309.50 ($57.46 × 75 people)	
Add 10% miscellaneous	22.72	Total $10,943.50	
Subtotal	$249.97		
Add 4.5% credit card fee	11.24		
Subtotal expenses per person	$ 261.21		
22% administrative fee	$ 57.46		
Total expenses per person	$318.67	**Registration fee**	$320.00

Advantages and Disadvantages
of the Four Methods of Cost Recovery

There is no one correct method of administrative fee cost recovery. Each method can be appropriate depending on the specific needs of the organization and its programs. In fact, some offices that plan many conferences, workshops, and meetings use different combinations of these methods according to the unique features of each program.

Flat Administrative Fee

The major advantage of the flat administrative fee is that it is a neat and clean way to recover administrative overhead. If you plan all the programs yourself and do not have to work with planning or advisory committees, this is probably the best and easiest method. However, if you are working with such committees, this method may be dysfunctional — especially if your office must be completely self-supporting. The reason for this is that to recover the true costs of your overhead, you may have to charge such a high flat administrative fee that it may scare people away from doing business with you, especially during preliminary discussions when they are deciding whether they wish to work with you.

Per Person Variable Fee

The per person variable fee is also a simple fee to establish and administer. You simply allocate a specific dollar amount to the per person variable fee column on the budget form. However, the total dollar amounts for all programs may not be enough to contribute what is necessary to cover your office overhead. This is especially true if the attendance for a number of programs falls considerably below your projections.

Percentage of Total Expenses

The percentage of total expenses method is also an easy cost recovery method to administer. However, if you are working with planning and advisory committees unfamiliar with true costs for running an office, they may balk at the percentage you charge. For example, if you need to charge 75 percent of all income for an administrative fee, groups unfamiliar with personnel and operating expenses may feel that this is excessive.

Combination Method

Using a combination of the three methods also has advantages and disadvantages. Its major advantage is that the specific dollar amounts related to each type administrative fees on the budget form may appear to be smaller than if only one method of cost recovery is used. The major disadvantage, if you have to work with planning and advisory committees, is that they may feel you have excessive cost recovery when they see two or three separate line items for this on a budget form. It is important to consider the specific needs of your organization and any clients with whom you have to work as part of the overall planning and running of any program. The administrative fee cost recovery should be designed to be compatible with the expectations of the organizational culture and still recover the kinds of expenses needed to pay for general office operating costs.

Summary

This chapter has summarized the four major ways in which general office overhead can be recovered through administrative fees charged to individual program budgets. A case study and actual budget forms illustrating each of the four types of cost recovery have been presented and analyzed. One of the most frequently made mistakes when using any type of cost recovery is that organizations fail to clearly establish the total dollar amount of general overhead expenses that programs must recover within a given fiscal year. Chapter Five shows how to do this. Until this is accomplished, any method of administrative fee cost recovery will probably prove to be ineffective.

The chapters thus far have concentrated on planning individual program budgets, identifying general overhead expenses for an office, and recovering administrative costs for a single conference, workshop, or meeting. The next chapter moves us further along in developing a comprehensive strategic financial management system.

5.

Developing
an Accounting System
That Enhances
Daily Decision Making

Use accrual accounting for all record keeping related to individual program budgets.

This chapter shows you how to set up an accounting system that will give you immediate and accurate access to the status of any individual program budget. The principles apply whether you are a one-person independent operation running your own business or a staff member in an office of a large parent organization.

If your office is a subunit of a larger parent organization that maintains an accounting system on a central computer, you probably automatically receive monthly printouts of your accounts. And like most people, you have probably learned to live with the fact that your monthly printouts are not much help in the daily financial management of specific programs. "Don't get me started on our central computerized accounting system," lament many leaders who plan conferences, workshops, and meetings. "Our reports lag three to four months behind what's happening in our accounts. For all practical purposes, our computer printouts are of no use whatsoever in helping us with daily decision making. You can't tell from the printouts what the actual balances are for any of our programs. In fact, a number of people on the staff feel that we'd be a lot better off using only hand record keeping. At least we'd know that it was accurate!"

Sound familiar? Other professionals who work in subunits of large parent organizations with central accounting systems often feel the same way. Centralized systems in a parent organization usually cannot provide up-to-the-minute data for assisting program managers with their daily financial decision making. There are two reasons why this is so.

First, most central accounting systems were not originally designed to provide accurate up-to-date information useful for daily decision making. Continuing to blame such a central accounting system for its ineffectiveness does not address the issue. Accounting systems can accomplish only what they were originally designed to do. Second, how records of income and expenses need to be kept varies widely from one department to another in a parent organization. Therefore, it is usually impossible to design a central accounting system that will meet the daily management needs of all individual departments. Large central accounting systems have usually been designed only to handle stewardship accounting. This they can do very well.

The Role of Stewardship Accounting

Central accounting systems have usually been designed with one main idea in mind — to show after the fact that money was spent as regulations say it should be spent. Six to twelve months after a program, the balance sheet will show that income was received and spent according to organizational regulations. Such a record-keeping system, designed to show after-the-fact proof of income and expenses, is known as *stewardship accounting*. Its main purpose is serving as a watchdog or *steward of funds*.

In most organizations, there are elaborate rules, conventions, guidelines, and sometimes even laws governing how money will be received and spent. In addition, there are usually elaborate formal procedures for keeping track of and documenting each monetary transaction. A steward of funds (the central accounting office) must be able to document that money has been received and spent according to the rules, guidelines, conventions, and laws adopted by the parent organization. As a result, most central accounting offices can provide very reliable after-the-fact documentation related to financial management. Therefore, stewardship accounting fulfills the organization's legal responsibilities for demonstrating that it is handling money properly.

Stewardship accounting means that much paperwork related to keeping track of money usually flows up and down the organizational chain of command. At each point in this flow, someone checks the paperwork and sends it on. This checking process takes a great deal of time. As a result, a computer printout of any individual account will often lag weeks or even months behind the actual balance in the account. The problem is that program managers need daily access to accurate financial records if they are to be able to make the best possible decisions on a day-to-day basis. The following case illustrates this problem.

Joan Worthington is a program director for a continuing education office in a large hospital. She has conducted a one-day program entitled Time Management for the Busy Health Care Executive. Her budget calls for the attendance of twenty-five people to break even with a registration fee of $200 each. Thus, her total projected income is $5,000.

During the two weeks after her program, Joan completes all the paperwork to pay eight individual bills related to this program. She sends the paperwork to the hospital's central accounting office at various times over the course of a two-week period. On her next monthly computer printout, Joan sees the information shown in Exhibit 5.1.

The illustration shows a balance of $3,065. However, Joan knows that this is not correct. She has sent to central accounting the paperwork to pay eight different bills, but only three of these bills have actually been posted on the monthly statement. Therefore, five additional bills have to be posted as expenses to her program.

"Oh, well," she thinks, "I'll just have to wait until next

Exhibit 5.1. Budget for a Time-Management Program.

Income			
Item	**Amount**		
Perking	$200	Leonard	$200
Wextler	200	Dixon	200
Johnson	200	Matthews	200
Mathers	200	Bowmaster	200
Smith	200	Crowley	200
Walton	200	McMahon	200
Zester	200	Rathje	200
Dresselhaus	200	Scheifelbein	200
Van Kekerix	200	Sherwood	200
Jenkins	200	Lockwood	200
Eversoll	200	Grafe	200
Emil	200	Milligan	200
Clark	200		
		Total	$5,000
Expenses			
Twenty-five lunches—			
Maple Hotel	($ 435)	Note: only three of the
Honorarium—Wilma Exter	($1,200)	eight bills have been
Travel—Wilma Exter	($ 300)	posted to the account.
Total	($1,935)		
Balance	$3,065		

month to find out where I stand." And then she adds, "You just can't depend on central accounting to keep you up to date."

This short case provides a concrete example of a major problem often faced by program planners who work in a parent organization with a large central accounting system that can provide only stewardship accounting. The monthly printouts such as the one in Exhibit 5.1 usually lag behind the reality of what has taken place in relation to the budget. In this case, for example, only three expense items have been posted to the account even though the program manager has closed out the account and sent all eight expense items to central accounting for payment. These three expense items are the 25 lunches ($435), the honorarium for Wilma Exter ($1,200), and travel for Wilma Exter ($300), for a total of $1,935. When all income has been received and all bills have been paid, the balance will be only $14, as shown in Exhibit 5.2.

These examples demonstrate the importance of two key issues facing program managers for conferences, workshops, and meetings. First, it is important to develop a reliable accounting system that can enhance daily decision making regarding financial management of individual programs. Second, it is important to have access to computer printouts of all income and expenses for individual programs that are up to date within the last twenty-four hours.

Maintaining a Separate Set of Books

Since the central accounting system in a parent organization is set up only for stewardship accounting, it can never provide up-to-date information regarding the status of all your accounts. Therefore, you must maintain a separate set of books on a personal computer in your own office. Rather than spending time lambasting the ineffectiveness of central accounting, acknowledge that it is in your best interests to maintain a separate set of books. Until you have quick and accurate access to the status of all program accounts whenever needed, it will never be possible to implement a comprehensive strategic financial management system.

Exhibit 5.2. Revised Budget for a Time-Management Program.

Income			
Item	**Amount**		
Perking	$200	Leonard	$200
Wextler	200	Dixon	200
Johnson	200	Matthews	200
Mathers	200	Bowmaster	200
Smith	200	Crowley	200
Walton	200	McMahon	200
Zester	200	Rathje	200
Dresselhaus	200	Scheifelbein	200
Van Kekerix	200	Sherwood	200
Jenkins	200	Lockwood	200
Eversoll	200	Grafe	200
Emil	200	Milligan	200
Clark	200		
		Total	$5,000
Expenses			
Twenty-five lunches —			
Maple Hotel	($ 435)		
Honorarium — Wilma Exter	(1,200)		
Travel — Wilma Exter	(300)		
Printing	(576)	Note: these additional	
Mailing	(512)	amounts will be posted on	
Graphic design	(178)	next month's statement.	
Advertising	(285)		
Administrative fee	(1,500)		
Total	($4,986)		
Balance	$14		

Maintaining a separate set of books is particularly important in an organization that does a large number of conferences, workshops, and meetings. Increased volume, both in numbers of programs and in money associated with these programs, increases the likelihood for substantial errors in the management of finances if this policy is not adopted.

The first step in designing a separate accounting system is to arrange for the posting of all income and expenses to every separate account entity once a day. If this is not done, you lose control of the financial planning and management process. To be a successful program planner, you must have quick and easy access to the status of any of your accounts.

As Exhibits 5.1 and 5.2 demonstrate, monthly statements may or may not reflect all income that has been received and all expenses that have been paid—or all paperwork that has been processed to initiate payment. You can be put at a great disadvantage if you do not have accurate financial information regarding that portion of your organization's budget for which you are responsible. Leaders who do not establish excellent systems for the daily management of finances will find it difficult to design successful strategies for the long-range management of finances.

Accounting Concepts for Success

No matter what the size of your operation, it is important to adopt the following three important accounting concepts that are critical to long-term success in strategic financial management.

Concept 1: Establish an Accrual Accounting System

Most large parent organizations use a cash rather than an accrual accounting system, although organizations rarely have a pure model of either system. To illustrate why accrual accounting and not cash accounting should be used, the following definitions and examples are important.

With *accrual accounting,* money is treated as income when it is earned, even though it may not actually have been received. Money to be paid out is treated as an expense whenever bills are incurred, even though bills for such expenses may not actually have been received or paid. This is the most effective accounting method for managing finances for conferences, workshops, and meetings. Illustrations later in the chapter demonstrate why this is so.

With *cash accounting,* money is treated as income only when it is received. Money going out of the organization is treated as an expense only when bills are actually paid. This is an unsuitable accounting system for managing conferences, workshops, and meetings. Cash accounting will give an inaccurate picture of the account until all income has actually been received and all bills have actually been paid.

The following case study and the accompanying exhibits demonstrate the difference between accrual accounting and cash accounting and show how cash accounting gives a misleading picture of the status of an account for individual programs.

Sam Dalton is a program manager in the Office of Training and Development of a large state government personnel department. He has planned and held a small workshop that needed fifteen registrants to break even. Twenty people registered and paid $125 each. All twenty registrants were paid for by departments in the state government. In addition, Sam received a $500 grant from the department's professional development fund to help pay expenses and thus keep the registration fee to $125. Because the workshop was small, he had only the following four bills to pay:

1. Printing—$300. This bill has not been received yet.
2. Postage—$350. This has not been paid because the mailing center has not yet sent him the bill.
3. Meals—$275. This bill will be paid as soon as it is received from the local hotel where the workshop was held. Sam hopes to receive this bill within three weeks.
4. Administrative fee—$1,500. This is the fee that needs to be recovered to pay for staff time to plan and administer the program. This bill has actually been paid through a budget transfer to the proper general office overhead account.

Sam's balance sheet will look very different depending on whether he uses a cash or an accrual accounting system. Exhibit 5.3 shows how the balance sheet will look using these two different accounting systems.

In accrual accounting, all registrants for the program have been counted as income even though some of the money for registration fees has not yet been received. The encumbrance column lists an X by the name of anyone whose money has not yet been received. This is the purpose of encumbering money — to account for it even though it has not yet been received. Similarly, three items in the expense category are listed as encumbrances. Sam knows the amount of these bills even though they have not yet been received. Using an accrual accounting system that notes encumbrances, a program manager can always maintain an accurate record of where any account should stand when it is closed out.

In cash accounting, income is posted only when it is actually received. Income is listed for only thirteen people, not the twenty people who actually attended, because the office has not yet received the money from the department paying their registration fees. Thus, it is apparent that the income figure is extremely misleading for the purposes of trying to determine how the account is actually going to turn out when all income is received and all expenses have been paid. Using a cash accounting system, a program manager cannot get an accurate picture of the status of a program account until all income has actually been received and all expenses have actually been paid. It often takes weeks or months for this to occur.

This illustration demonstrates why cash accounting does not give program managers an accurate picture of the status of an individual program budget. Using an accrual accounting system, Sam knows his final balance will be $575. However, using a cash accounting system, his balance is shown as $1,325. If Sam manages only one program, this may not prove to be a problem, since he probably can quickly do hand calculations to determine his final balance. However, if he does many programs during a year, constantly doing hand calculations is not practical.

Exhibit 5.3. Accrual Versus Cash Accounting.

Accrual accounting			Cash accounting		
Income	Amount	Encumber	Income	Amount	
Edwards	$ 125	X	Gifford	$125	
Liberty	125	X	Adams	125	
Aden	125	X	Mullford	125	
Benson	125	X	Maxwell	125	
Gifford	125		Gamble	125	
Adams	125		Jones	125	
Mullford	125		West	125	
Maxwell	125		Blumberg	125	
Sanders	125	X	Sorrenson	125	
Gamble	125		Gelason	125	
Jones	125		Gilbertson	125	
West	125		Paxton	125	
Josephs	125	X	Falks	125	
Zander	125	X			
Blumberg	125				
Sorrenson	125				
Gelason	125				
Gilbertson	125				
Anderson	125				
Falks	125				
Professional					
development fund	500	X			
Total income	**$3,000**	X	**Total income**	**$1,625**	
Expenses			Expenses		
Printing	($ 300)	X	Printing	($300)	
Postage	(350)	X			
Meals — hotel	(275)	X			
Administrative fee	(1,500)				
Total expenses	**($2,425)**		**Total expenses**	**($300)**	
Balance	**$575**		**Balance**	**$1,325**	

Concept 2: Establish a Reliable Encumbrance System

Encumbrances are used extensively in accrual accounting. Encumbering money is a method for formally noting that specific income is expected or specific expenses have been incurred. For example, from the figures in Exhibit 5.2, Sam knows that all twenty registrants will eat lunch. By getting a quotation from the hotel ahead of time, he knows that the entire cost of the lunch will be $275, even though he has not yet actually received the bill. Thus, on a balance sheet, he encumbers, or earmarks, money to pay this expense when he receives the official bill. Similarly, Sam knows that he is going to receive $500 from the professional development fund to assist with expenses. Therefore, he notes this fact with an X in the encumbrance column under income. Sam also puts an X beside the name of each registrant who has not paid; bills have been sent, and he knows that he will receive the money. Then as income is actually received and as expenses are actually paid, the X in the encumbrance column is removed.

Concept 3: Implement Fund Accounting

Income and expenses from different programs should never be commingled. To ensure that this does not happen, it is necessary to develop a fund accounting system. Fund accounting is particularly useful for offices planning conferences, workshops, and meetings. Fund accounting divides the money for the entire office into appropriate separate accounts or funds. For example, each conference, workshop, or meeting has its own separate account number or fund. This enables income and expenses to be posted to the appropriate account. Setting up a fund of accounts is as simple as assigning a separate account number to each conference, workshop, or meeting and establishing a separate account for general office overhead expenses. This makes it easy to assign income and expenses to the appropriate individual account number. Then, whether you use a hand or a computerized bookkeeping system, it is easy to track income and expenses for individual programs. Fund accounting should always be used for conferences, workshops, and meetings. The next chapter contains exhibits showing how to separate individual programs or funds for accounting purposes.

Summary

This chapter has described how to institute a decentralized accounting system that helps program planners with their daily decision making related to strategic financial management. Regardless of the size of an office or how many conferences, workshops, and meetings are planned, the principles presented in this chapter are the same. If yours is a subunit of a large parent organization, you will probably have to keep a separate set of books to have access to the most up-to-date information regarding the status of all your different accounts. It is easy to maintain this separate set of books on a personal computer using one of the many sophisticated software packages available to assist with financial management. (See Resource C for suggestions on computer software.)

Developing this type of internal, decentralized accounting system is an empowering process for staff. It gives eveyone access to accurate financial information regarding the status of any account. Thus, program managers are able to do an excellent job at managing all their accounts. This, in turn, helps the office achieve a level of excellence impossible without this type of system.

6.

Planning
the Comprehensive
Strategic Financial Management
System

It is important to conceptualize strategic financial management as a long-term project. Use electronic spreadsheets to create a five-year budget.

Attendance at conferences, workshops, and meetings is affected by a wide variety of variables, including the program topic, the amount of the registration fee, weather, location, long-term shifts in marketing, and shifts in attitudes toward the topic or the sponsoring organization. Any one of these variables or several acting together can affect financial success of the program. How, then, can one develop ways to maximize overall financial success for the office? This can be done by creating a comprehensive strategic financial management system. Developing such a system makes it possible to discuss, debate, and analyze alternative scenarios. In addition, it allows for assessment of risk for individual programs and the office in general.

Previous chapters have illustrated how to develop a budget for a single program, how to develop a budget to cover general overhead expenses, and how to recover general overhead expenses through charging administrative fees back to individual program budgets. This chapter shows how to use electronic spreadsheets on personal computers to create a comprehensive strategic financial planning process. The chapter also addresses the most common mistakes made in developing this type of computerized strategic financial management system. It shows how to project general office overhead expenses five years into the future as a way of planning for long-range administrative fee cost recovery. In addition, it shows how to gain control over the long-range strategic financial planning process by displaying an office's five-year projection of anticipated income and expenses. This enables staff to become better at planning specific strategies for long-term financial success.

Using the principles, guidelines, and budget planning formats suggested in this chapter, it is possible to bring comprehensive strategic financial management to any office engaged in the work of conferences, workshops, and meetings. The system of using electronic spreadsheets on personal computers described in this chapter establishes basic principles and guidelines to be followed in planning your own system. Naturally, it is important to adapt these principles to meet the requirements of your own organization.

Creating Alternative Financial Management Scenarios

An essential part of developing a comprehensive strategic financial management system is using electronic spreadsheets to project income and expenses into the future. This makes it possible to create alternative budget scenarios for individual programs as well as for the total office budget. These scenarios display financial data accurately and logically so that individuals and management teams can discuss, debate, analyze, and create models of possible alternative courses of action before they are actually implemented.

There are two main benefits of this scenario-creation process. First, it enables staff to consider a wide variety of alternative strategies for all aspects of strategic financial management, simulating the consequences of different possible decisions. Debating and analyzing these potential decisions can stimulate creative thinking among management teams, generating alternatives that may not previously have been considered.

Second, creating alternative scenarios enables individuals and management teams to enhance their effectiveness by actively designing a successful financial future for their programs and for the office in general. This can be an empowering process that encourages all staff to develop a strong psychological commitment to the long-term success of the organization. This process of creating and analyzing alternative scenarios gives teams of people a stake in the ultimate financial success of the office.

Developing a Computerized
Strategic Financial Management System

At first glance, personal computers and the electronic spreadsheets that they can generate seem to be the answer to many problems associated with implementing strategic financial management. However, it is easy to be fooled by computer printouts. The data printed on spreadsheets looks very official. They are organized in handsome-looking columns and rows. However, as with all computerized accounting and planning systems, the data are only as reliable as the assumptions underlying the numbers. Therefore, before implementing any computerized strategic financial management system, it is important to consider the following issues.

First, personal computers and their accompanying electronic spreadsheets have revolutionized the way we do business. Today, laptop computers have the power of computers that needed an entire room to house a few years ago. The power and sophistication of personal computers and their software are growing at exponential rates. It is safe to assume that in another few years, educational program planners who do not know how to use computer software packages to handle a wide variety of management tasks in their organizations will be virtually unemployable. In fact, in many organizations that plan conferences, workshops, and meetings, this is already the case.

Second, you should never try to computerize an accounting and financial planning system that does not work effectively with manual record keeping. Any record-keeping system must provide an effective way to plan an accurate budget for individual programs. It must establish an administrative fee cost recovery for all programs using one of the methods described in previous chapters. In addition, it is important to display data from income and expenses for all programs so that it is easy for everyone responsible for the daily management of programs to understand the budgeting and strategic financial management system. Only when all of these elements work effectively in a hand record-keeping system should the process be transferred to a computer.

There are six important steps that leaders who plan conferences, workshops, and meetings should take when designing a comprehensive strategic financial management system. First, project all general office expenses and income for a five-year period and display them on an electronic spreadsheet. Second, identify and display detailed summary budget data for a total year of programs. Third, sort this summary of the one-year schedule of program income and expenses by individual program director. Fourth, balance income and expenses from all programs against the total general office expenses for overhead. Fifth, identify alternative courses of action for dealing with problem areas that emerge as a result of this financial modeling. Sixth, decide on appropriate action steps and implement them. The case study that follows analyzes the first three of these steps; the remaining three steps are discussed in Chapter Seven.

Case Study: First Steps in Developing a Strategic Financial Management Plan

The setting for the case study here is an office in a large university on the East Coast. However, the strategic financial management principles highlighted in the case apply to any office that organizes conferences, workshops, and meetings, no matter what its size or mission. The principles are the same whether you are working in the for-profit or the not-for-profit sector.

Marion Johnson has recently taken a job as director of the Office of Conferences and Institutes in a large university. Marion supervises a team of three program managers plus four support personnel. The mission of the office is to develop conferences, workshops, and meetings that will support the outreach efforts of the university. The office tries to maximize its program development efforts by offering its programs in a number of different locations besides the city where the university is located.

While the office is designed to be completely self-supporting, it has had an uneven financial history. For the last three years, the office has lost more than $100,000 per year. Marion was hired to put the office on an even financial keel and make it truly self-supporting. This responsibility was made very clear to her during the interview process. On taking up her new position, Marion found that there was a great deal of conflict among the staff regarding what was needed to become completely self-supporting. "If the books were kept correctly," one staff member told Marion, "we'd be self-supporting. But I wouldn't trust our accounting system as far as I could throw it. And believe me, I'd like to throw it — right out the window. It stinks! I can never tell where I stand regarding the income and expenses in any of my accounts."

Marion found that the office relied exclusively on the monthly budget printouts from the university's central accounting office for data on the status of income and expenses for all programs. The team of program managers had never seen a copy of a budget for the entire office. In fact, one program manager noted, "I've never seen an accurate copy of a budget for any of my own programs. I can't count on our accounting office for any kind of statement that can actually help me with my daily decision making."

The office was already using a budget planning form similar to the one recommended in this book. However, the budget form was always filled out by hand or with a typewriter. The form was not programmed on an electronic spreadsheet so that data could be easily and quickly changed to create alternative budget scenarios as individual programs were being planned.

Neither was there any type of computer printout summarizing the projected income and expenses for all programs handled by the office during the current fiscal year.

Marion wanted to bring a team approach to problem solving for the office. However, it was hard to bring a concept of team problem solving to the situation when the team had never seen a reliable set of coherently organized data about the office's entire budget. Therefore, Marion decided that the first priority would be to create such a set of logically organized data. She also decided to present the data in a clear visual format that would help promote discussion, analysis, and team problem solving.

The illustrations, discussion, and analysis that follow show how Marion went about doing this. Marion had a clear goal in mind: to implement a comprehensive strategic financial management system that would enable the office to break even.

Step 1: Display a Five-Year Projection of Expenses

Exhibit 6.1 displays the budget for general office overhead for Marion's office. Note that the form lists personnel expenses separately from general operating expenses. This makes it easy to apply the total fringe benefit rate to all personnel expenses. The spreadsheet is then programmed to automatically recalculate the subtotal of personnel expenses and fringe benefits so that the total expenses for personnel can easily be identified. Changing any number on the spreadsheet will automatically recalculate all key totals and display the correct grand total for all general office expenses. Below the figures for personnel expenses, operating expenses projected to be incurred during the coming year are listed on a line-by-line basis. Note that any expenses that can be attributed to a specific conference, workshop, or meeting are not included in this list.

After identifying all personnel and operating expenses, Marion has added a miscellaneous amount to the total expenses. Many offices similar to Marion's find that they need to add a line item of at least 10 percent for miscellaneous expenses. Often known as "wiggle room" or the "fudge factor," this projected line item is designed to cover unforeseen expenses that always emerge in any office during the course of a fiscal year.

The expenses listed in column A are for the current year. Expenses listed in columns B through E assume a 4 percent increase every year for each line item. This figure can be changed to fit the special needs of different organizations. Using the spreadsheet, you can easily create additional budget scenarios that ask "What if?" questions. What if personnel costs increase 4 percent, but operating costs increase 5 percent? What if telephone expenses increase 8 percent, but travel expenses decrease by 2 percent? What if some personnel get 3 percent raises, while others get 4 percent raises?

Always take a long-term approach to financial planning. When the budget for a fiscal year has been developed, project it into the future so that a five-year budget can be conceptualized during discussions. This helps staff realize that budget planning is a dynamic, constantly changing process. Decisions involving any individual program budget almost always have long-term implications for the office. For example, if an individual program loses money, this will probably affect the amount that is recovered for administrative fees to pay for general office expenses.

When the budget is complete, share the spreadsheet with staff so they can understand the total budget. This helps create the best possible team problem solving. Staff may spot categories where money can be saved, identify items where expenses have been underestimated, or find an incorrect dollar amount that has been entered on a particular line. It is through this type of team problem solving that all staff are able to contribute to long-term strategic financial management.

Step 2: Display Summary Budget Data for One Year of Programs

After a five-year budget projecting general office expenses has been created, a summary of all income and expenses for individual programs during a fiscal year should be prepared. This summary is based on the budgeting information found on the budget forms for individual conferences, workshops, and meetings. Exhibit 6.2 shows how to display these data.

Exhibit 6.1. General Office Overhead.

	A	B	C	D	E
	Year 1	Year 2	Year 3	Year 4	Year 5
		4% increase	4% increase	4% increase	4% increase
Personnel expenses					
Johnson	$ 65,736	$ 68,365	$ 71,100	$ 73,944	$ 76,902
Wexler	56,867	59,142	61,507	63,968	66,526
Nattleson	45,345	47,159	49,045	51,007	53,047
Defter	47,989	49,909	51,905	53,981	56,140
Baxter	25,760	26,790	27,862	28,976	30,136
Weston	20,800	21,632	22,497	23,397	24,333
Blexon	21,456	22,314	23,207	24,135	25,100
Winston	22,967	23,886	24,841	25,835	26,868
Subtotal	$306,920	$319,197	$331,965	$345,243	$359,053
Fringes @ 25%	76,730	79,799	82,991	86,311	89,763
Subtotal	**$383,650**	$398,996	$414,956	$431,554	$448,816

Operating expenses	A	B	C	D	E
Custodial	$ 3,545	$ 3,687	$ 3,834	$ 3,988	$ 4,147
Supplies	9,500	9,880	10,275	10,686	11,114
Equipment	11,000	11,440	11,898	12,374	12,868
Travel	8,000	8,320	8,653	8,999	9,359
Phones	6,000	6,240	6,490	6,749	7,019
Maintenance	6,385	6,640	6,906	7,182	7,470
Postage	17,900	18,616	19,361	20,135	20,940
Printing	8,000	8,320	8,653	8,999	9,359
Subtotal	$70,330	$73,143	$76,069	$79,112	$82,276
Total	$453,980	$472,139	$491,025	$510,666	$531,092
Plus 10% miscellaneous	45,398	47,214	49,102	51,067	53,109
Grand total	$499,378	$519,353	$540,127	$561,732	$584,202

For the purposes of projecting an inflation factor each year, each item will be increased each year by 4%. However, this percentage could be changed for any cell on this spreadsheet.

Note: With this general budget for the office, all expenses for individual conferences, workshops, or meetings are charged to a specific program with its own separate account number. Thus, instituting fund accounting is an important part of strategic financial management. Items listed above, such as printing and postage, are for general office expenses that cannot be attributed to any specific program.

Exhibit 6.2. Fiscal Year Program Summary Budget.

A	B	C	D	E	F	G	H
Person	Code	Program title	Income	Expenses	Administrative fee	Balance	Recovery
A	658	Computer Camp	$ 18,623	$ 6,254	$ 3,000	$ 12,369	$ 15,369
C	164	Communication Skills	23,612	19,258	3,000	4,354	7,354
A	610	Music Camp 1	28,460	23,561	2,000	4,899	6,899
B	786	Building Codes	68,900	36,000	25,000	32,900	57,900
A	435	Dance Symposium	58,464	45,084	6,500	13,380	19,880
C	318	History of Opera	26,002	18,645	4,500	7,357	11,857
A	588	Computer Programming	64,584	47,500	25,360	17,084	42,444
B	752	Water Resources	30,890	19,824	5,500	11,066	16,566
B	221	Swine Health	130,555	109,845	25,000	20,710	45,710
A	584	Intensive Spanish	35,600	7,000	6,000	28,600	34,600
B	985	Update on Tax Laws	78,625	25,000	15,000	53,625	68,625
C	582	Music Camp 2	36,548	15,410	2,000	21,138	23,138
C	879	Understanding Ballet	33,512	17,826	3,000	15,686	18,686
B	266	Tour to England	35,848	11,851	2,500	23,997	26,497
C	334	Business Accounting	21,645	16,384	3,000	5,261	8,261
A	647	Engineering Update	15,484	18,065	2,000	(2,581)	(581)
C	310	Computer Graphics	26,588	25,982	7,800	606	8,406
		Totals	$733,940	$463,489	$141,160	$270,451	$411,611

In Column A of the exhibit, an appropriate code is assigned to each program director. This code can be used to sort data according to the programs assigned to individual directors. (Later in the chapter, we see how this sorted information is displayed.) Column B contains the individual account numbers assigned to the programs. With separate account numbers, all income and expenses for each program can be accounted for separately. This is known as fund accounting. Moneys from one fund are never commingled with moneys in another fund. Column C shows the name of each program for easy identification. Program names are often abbreviated to fit into the space allocated for the program title on the spreadsheet.

Column D summarizes income from each program. For programs that have not yet taken place, this represents the estimated income from the budget forms for those programs. For programs that have taken place, this represents the actual income received using accrual accounting procedures.

Column E shows the total expenses for each program — estimated expenses for programs that have not yet taken place and actual expenses for programs that have. Column F identifies the total administrative fee cost recovery for each program. This administrative fee may be recovered in one of the four basic ways discussed earlier. Note that the administrative fee charged back to each program is included as part of the total expenses in Column E as well as being listed separately in Column F for easy identification.

Column G shows the positive or negative balance in the account. Figures in parentheses indicate negative balances, meaning that the final close-out of the budget produced an overall loss. A positive balance indicates that the program recovered its administrative fee listed in column F and made the additional amount listed in column G. Note that the administrative fee is always considered a direct expense item as money is tracked on this type of electronic spreadsheet.

Column H accounts for positive or negative balances in each account after all income has been received and all expenses, including the administrative fee in column F, have been paid. The $411,611 total in this column is the money available to offset the general office expenses of $499,378 found in Exhibit 6.1, column A.

It is essential to lay out an entire year's listing of programs in this manner in order to engage the team in a logical analysis of the entire budget for the office. This type of spreadsheet makes it easy to determine at any time the status of the total money available to offset general office expenses. When we pull these figures together from Exhibits 6.1 and 6.2, this is what the balance sheet looks like:

General office expenses (Exhibit 6.1)	$(499,378)
Total expected cost recovery (Exhibit 6.2)	$411,611
Balance	$(87,767)

Taking corrective action to eliminate this projected budget deficit of $87,767 is addressed in the next chapter.

Step 3: Sort Summary Data by Program Director

The next step is to sort the total list of programs into groups according to individual program directors, as illustrated in Exhibit 6.3. This makes it possible to analyze what each program director is contributing to the overall cost recovery for the office and thus to analyze work load. For example, we note that program director A contributes a total cost recovery of $118,611, program director B contributes $215,298, and program director C contributes $77,702. Of course, the dollar amount contributed by each program director to the general office overhead is not necessarily the only criterion that should be used to measure his or her success. There may be many good and justifiable reasons why one program manager contributed more than another toward offsetting the general office expenses.

For example, one of the programs may be a large international conference that has taken three years to plan. The office may have decided several years ago to contribute staff planning time to this endeavor because of its perceived importance to the parent organization. Thus, the administrative fee actually charged as a direct expense against the conference may be lower

Exhibit 6.3. Summary Program Budget by Program Director.

A	B	C	D	E	F	G	H
Person	Code	Program title	Income	Expenses	Administrative fee	Balance	Recovery
A	658	Computer Camp	$ 18,623	$ 6,254	$ 3,000	$ 12,369	$ 15,369
A	610	Music Camp 1	28,460	23,561	2,000	4,899	6,899
A	435	Dance Symposium	58,464	45,084	6,500	13,380	19,880
A	588	Computer Programming	64,584	47,500	25,360	17,084	42,444
A	584	Intensive Spanish	35,600	7,000	6,000	28,600	34,600
A	647	Engineering Update	15,484	18,065	2,000	(2,581)	(581)
		Subtotals	**$221,215**	**$147,464**	**$44,860**	**$73,751**	**$118,611**
B	786	Building Codes	68,900	36,000	25,000	32,900	57,900
B	752	Water Resources	30,890	19,824	5,500	11,066	16,566
B	221	Swine Health	130,555	109,845	25,000	20,710	45,710
B	985	Update on Tax Laws	78,625	25,000	15,000	53,625	68,625
B	266	Tour to England	35,848	11,851	2,500	23,997	26,497
		Subtotals	**$334,818**	**$202,520**	**$73,000**	**$142,298**	**$215,298**
C	164	Communication Skills	23,612	19,258	3,000	4,354	7,354
C	318	History of Opera	26,002	18,645	4,500	7,357	11,857
C	582	Music Camp 2	36,548	15,410	2,000	21,138	23,138
C	879	Understanding Ballet	33,512	17,826	3,000	15,686	18,686
C	334	Business Accounting	21,645	16,384	3,000	5,261	8,261
C	310	Computer Graphics	26,588	25,982	7,800	606	8,406
		Subtotals	**$167,907**	**$113,505**	**$23,300**	**$54,402**	**$77,702**
		Totals	**$733,940**	**$463,489**	**$141,160**	**$270,451**	**$411,611**

than the actual cost of staff time required to plan it. Presumably, all the appropriate key players would have agreed to this financial arrangement before it was implemented. Further, given the unpredictability of the marketplace, some programs may not have drawn the number of registrants that had been projected. Or a program manager may have been assigned to the office only part-time and would therefore not be expected to carry as heavy a load as full-time program managers. Of course, it may simply be that some program planners are not meeting reasonable organizational expectations regarding work load. Whatever the problem, without a spreadsheet like the one shown in Exhibit 6.3, it will be difficult to even conceptualize it. With such a spreadsheet, the team will be able to work from a reliable common data base to guide discussions and analysis.

Summary

The office described in the case study in this chapter is now well on its way to implementing a system of comprehensive strategic financial management. All the component parts have been put into place. Individual programs are planned according to an agreed-on process that is used by everyone in the office. Budget forms clearly distinguish between fixed and variable expenses and clearly identify administrative fees. Electronic spreadsheets display summary budget information for all programs. This information can easily be sorted by individual program director. And the budget planning process is carried out a year at a time so that early warning systems will identify potential overall financial problems. For example, according to the data the office is projected to run a deficit. The next chapter demonstrates alternative ways in which Marion and the staff can go about addressing this issue.

7.

Using
a Team Approach
to Create
a Balanced Budget

Good budget planning must always deal with the reality of your entire financial situation.

If Marion and the staff in the Office of Conferences and Institutes had not created the series of spreadsheets shown in Chapter Six, they would not be able to determine that their office is in financial trouble. It is always a shock to learn that you have serious financial problems. However, there is hope, as we will see during the continued analysis of this case. With their spreadsheets, the program managers now have important financial data that are clearly and logically organized. This will assist the team in moving to the next phase of implementing a comprehensive strategic financial management system for the office.

Completing the Six Steps

This section describes the last three of the six steps necessary in developing an overall plan for strategic financial management as presented in Chapter Six.

Step 4: Balance Program Income and
Expenses Against General Office Overhead

The spreadsheets in Chapter Six present the relevant figures for the Office of Conferences and Institutes. The overall financial picture for the office is as follows:

General office expenses (Exhibit 6.1)	($499,378)
Total cost recovery (column H, Exhibit 6.2)	$411,611
Balance	($87,767)

As the figures show, the office is projecting a deficit of $87,767 for the fiscal year. With this projected deficit clearly at the forefront of all financial planning discussions, the team addresses this issue immediately.

Step 5: Identify Alternative Courses of Action

Because the financial situation is so serious, Marion and the three program managers decide to devote an entire day to a staff meeting analyzing this problem. They get together in their conference room to review and analyze all the spreadsheets. As they discuss alternative courses of action, one program manager comments, "We've never done this type of planning before. I've always just been told the formula for recovering administrative fees. Then when the office ran a deficit, they hauled me in and raked me over the coals for an hour or so, but then I went on and did my programs. There were no negative consequences for running a deficit other than getting a stern lecture."

The group decides to create a list of all the possible alternative courses of action and lists them on a flip chart so that everyone can see them. They decide to focus on the following five major alternatives:

1. *Make a specific plan to reduce expenses by $87,767.* Note that using this option means taking *specific steps* to eliminate the $87,767 in expenses. Good intentions to do something about

the deficit do not substitute for appropriate quantifiable action. The steps taken must be quantifiable so that they can be reflected on an electronic spreadsheet that shows a completely balanced budget. Until this happens, the staff will not be using strategic financial management but will simply be thinking about some possible alternatives.

2. *Create enough new programs to cover the projected deficit through additional administrative fees and cost recovery.* This alternative may be useful if the projected deficit is highlighted early in the year. However, if it is not discovered until later in the fiscal year, it may be too late to implement this alternative.

3. *Negotiate with the parent organization to pick up part or all of the projected deficit.* Before this is done, the entire conference operation should be carefully reviewed to determine what benefits will accrue to the parent organization if it subsidizes the program. For example, if a subsidy is requested to take care of the deficit without a concrete plan for addressing the problems that have caused it, the parent organization probably will not be receptive to such a suggestion.

4. *Use a combination of the first three approaches.* Under this plan, the staff would reduce expenses, create new programs, and request that the parent organization cover part of the deficit until the next year, when they can sort out their financial situation.

When a budget deficit is finally faced, it may be easy to become optimistic and quickly develop a positive budget scenario on paper. However, this process should also include a careful and detailed analysis of how the budget deficit occurred. There may be complex problems or issues related to overall planning and financial management that have to be addressed to avoid future deficits. It is not the responsibility of the parent organization to force the conference operation to address the deficit budgeting issues. Rather, it is the responsibility of the Office of Conferences and Institutes to devise a comprehensive strategic financial planning system that will enable the office to break even.

As a result of the day-long session in the conference room, Marion and the staff realize that they must take specific immediate steps to address the problem of the projected deficit. Waiting several months in the hope that things will work themselves out as a result of an upswing in the economy is not a responsible approach. They must choose from one of the above four options and implement that option immediately in specific, measurable ways that can be accounted for in a new scenario. It is important that this new scenario be displayed on an electronic spreadsheet so that everyone can see and discuss the factors involved. This will encourage the best possible team decision making. Painful choices are often involved in balancing a budget.

Now let us follow Marion and the management team through the next two weeks as they take specific steps to eliminate the projected deficit of $87,767. The staff quickly decide to develop the following new programs to be offered during the current fiscal year: Financial Management for Nonaccountants, Symposium on Gerontology, Strategic Planning for Managers, and Increased Global Exports.

After developing individual budgets for each of these four programs, they plug the new financial figures into the electronic spreadsheet displaying the year's programs, as shown in the shaded areas of Exhibit 7.1. Marion and the staff now quickly recalculate the status of the office budget for the fiscal year as follows:

General office expenses (Exhibit 6.1)	($499,378)
Total expected cost recovery (column H, Exhibit 7.1)	$468,385
Balance	($30,993)

By creating the four new programs, they have reduced their projected deficit from $87,767 to $30,993.

Step 6: Identify and Implement Appropriate Action Steps

The team feels better about their finances now that they have developed the new programs and planned their budgets. However,

Exhibit 7.1. Amended Fiscal Year Program Summary Budget.

A	B	C	D	E	F	G	H
Person	Code	Program title	Income	Expenses	Administrative fee	Balance	Recovery
A	658	Computer Camp	$ 18,623	$ 6,254	$ 3,000	$ 12,369	$ 15,369
C	164	Communication Skills	23,612	19,258	3,000	4,354	7,354
A	610	Music Camp 1	28,460	23,561	2,000	4,899	6,899
B	786	Building Codes	68,900	36,000	25,000	32,900	57,900
A	435	Dance Symposium	58,464	45,084	6,500	13,380	19,880
C	318	History of Opera	26,002	18,645	4,500	7,357	11,857
A	588	Computer Programming	64,584	47,500	25,360	17,084	42,444
B	752	Water Resources	30,890	19,824	5,500	11,066	16,566
B	221	Swine Health	130,555	109,845	25,000	20,710	45,710
A	584	Intensive Spanish	35,600	7,000	6,000	28,600	34,600
B	985	Update on Tax Laws	78,625	25,000	15,000	53,625	68,625
C	582	Music Camp 2	36,548	15,410	2,000	21,138	23,138
C	879	Understanding Ballet	33,512	17,826	3,000	15,686	18,686
B	266	Tour to England	35,848	11,851	2,500	23,997	26,497
C	334	Business Accounting	21,645	16,384	3,000	5,261	8,261
A	647	Engineering Update	15,484	18,065	2,000	(2,581)	(581)
C	310	Computer Graphics	26,588	25,982	7,800	606	8,406
A	777	Financial/Nonaccountants	68,374	68,000	5,000	374	5,374
B	47	Symposium/Gerontology	21,900	20,000	8,000	1,900	9,900
C	465	Strategic Planning	49,000	47,000	9,500	2,000	11,500
A	980	Global Exports	86,000	76,000	20,000	10,000	30,000
		Totals	$959,214	$674,489	$183,660	$284,725	$468,385

they are still projecting a $30,993 deficit. Therefore, they decide to take the following additional actions. Marion makes an appointment with the dean of continuing education, to whom she reports, and goes over her figures with the dean. The dean agrees to underwrite $10,000 of the projected losses for this year only. The dean realizes that Marion is new and is trying very hard to turn around the financial planning in the Office of Conferences and Institutes but emphasizes that next year it will not be possible to underwrite any losses for the office.

"You need to know this up front," says the dean. "I am able to help you for this year. However, we must be very clear on our agreement. I will not be able to underwrite any of your losses next year. Therefore, beginning today, you will need to give special attention to planning next year's series of programs. You will also need to give careful attention to planning your general office expenses for this year and next year. You probably will have to reduce some expenses in this area if you cannot generate enough additional income through programs to cover your general office expenses."

Marion leaves the dean's office somewhat relieved. The $10,000 underwriting is more than she had hoped for. Returning to her office, Marion plugs this new figure into her electronic spreadsheet and updates the projections to determine how much more must be cut from the budget. The new calculations are as follows:

General office expenses (Exhibit 6.1)	($499,378)
Total expected cost recovery (column H, Exhibit 7.1)	$468,385
Contribution from the dean	$10,000
Balance	($20,993)

Marion and the staff now have a projected deficit of only $20,993. Things are looking better, but they still need to completely balance their budget. Marion calls the three program managers together to analyze the latest version of the total office budget. They all confirm that the individual program budgets for which they are responsible contain the most realistic projections possible at this time, and they still have a $20,993 problem.

Next comes one of the most difficult parts of creating alternative scenarios to eliminate the deficit. The picture is now very clear to Marion and the staff: the office budget for general overhead will have to be reduced by $20,993. There are no logical alternatives. After much discussion, Marion and the staff decide on the only responsible course of action to represent the best interests of their organization. They will have to make cuts. They agree to eliminate one secretarial position. This is the position of Bev Weston, who makes $20,800 plus 25 percent fringe benefits for a total of $26,000. Thus, the new budget scenario now looks like this:

General office expenses (Exhibit 6.1)	($499,378)
Total expected cost recovery (column H, Exhibit 7.1)	$468,385
Contribution from the dean	$10,000
Eliminate secretary	$26,000
Balance	$5,007

Now they are projecting a positive balance of $5,007. After much discussion, the team also decides to reduce their travel expenses by $4,000. Their reasoning is that this is one item that they can easily control. In addition, they decide to postpone purchasing an additional printer for their computers. This will save an additional $2,000. Thus, the next version of their budget looks like this:

General office expenses (Exhibit 6.1)	($499,378)
Total expected cost recovery (column H, Exhibit 7.1)	$468,385
Contribution from the dean	$10,000
Eliminate secretary	$26,000
Reduce travel	$4,000
Reduce equipment purchases	$2,000
Balance	$11,007

Now the budget shows a positive projected balance of $11,007. This positive balance leaves additional "wiggle room" in the budget. If this budget plays itself out as projected during the course of a year, this means that the $10,000 contribution from the dean will not be needed. The new budget reflecting the budget reductions projected for five years is shown in Exhibit 7.2.

Exhibit 7.2. Amended General Office Overhead.

	A Year 1	B Year 2 4% increase	C Year 3 4% increase	D Year 4 4% increase	E Year 5 4% increase
Personnel					
Johnson	$ 65,736	$ 68,365	$ 71,100	$ 73,944	$ 76,902
Wexler	56,867	59,142	61,507	63,968	66,526
Nattleson	45,345	47,159	49,045	51,007	53,047
Defter	47,989	49,909	51,905	53,981	56,140
Baxter	25,760	26,790	27,862	28,976	30,136
Blexon	21,456	22,314	23,207	24,135	25,100
Winston	22,967	23,886	24,841	25,835	26,868
Staff Reduction (Weston)	0	0	0	0	0
Subtotal	$286,120	$297,565	$309,467	$321,846	$334,720
Fringes @ 25%	71,530	74,391	77,367	80,462	83,680
Subtotal	$357,650	$371,956	$386,834	$402,308	$418,400

Operating	A	B	C	D	E
Custodial	$ 3,545	$ 3,687	$ 3,834	$ 3,988	$ 4,147
Supplies	9,500	9,880	10,275	10,686	11,114
Equipment	9,000	9,360	9,734	10,124	10,529
Travel	4,000	4,160	4,326	4,499	4,679
Phones	6,000	6,240	6,490	6,749	7,019
Maintenance	6,385	6,640	6,906	7,182	7,470
Postage	17,900	18,616	19,361	20,135	20,940
Printing	8,000	8,320	8,653	8,999	9,359
Subtotal	$ 64,330	$ 66,903	$ 69,579	$72,363	$ 75,257
Total	$421,980	438,859	456,414	474,670	493,657
Plus 10% miscellaneous	42,198	43,886	45,641	47,467	49,336
Grand total	$464,178	$482,745	$502,055	$522,137	$543,023
For the purposes of projecting an inflation factor each year, all line items are increased 4% each year. However, any dollar amount in any cell on the spreadsheet could be changed to reflect a different percentage increase.					

Note: In this illustration, the salary of Bev Weston, along with her fringe benefits for a total of $26,000, has been eliminated. In addition, equipment purchases have been reduced by $2,000 for a total of $9,000. Travel has been reduced from $8,000 to $4,000.

The spreadsheet in Exhibit 7.2 shows the complete office budget with the newly identified reductions. The five-year budget projection is automatically adjusted in the spreadsheet to reflect the budget reductions. The data are presented in a clear, logical manner that makes them easy to comprehend. This contributes to productive discussion, analysis, and problem solving. If there are any errors in the data, the team members should be able to catch them, since everyone has access to the same information. As the budget is updated during the year, additional alternative scenarios can easily be created to deal with the changing figures as programs are held and their budgets closed out. Thus, creating the type of alternative financial scenarios presented in this chapter makes it easy for Marion and the team to engage in sophisticated financial planning.

Summary

Long-range strategic financial management emphasizes the long-term health of the organization. The focus on team problem solving means that all members of the team are given access to all budget information related to the office as well as to individual programs. The team is actively involved in creating alternative courses of action that can be used to balance the budget and encouraged to take definite actions as they choose among alternative scenarios. These actions must result in a balanced budget as projected on the electronic spreadsheets. Through this process, team members develop a strong commitment to creating success for themselves and their organization.

The chapters to this point have presented principles and guidelines for implementing the mechanics of a comprehensive strategic financial management system. The next two chapters deal with the human, political, and organizational factors that affect strategic financial management.

8.

Seven Principles
That Ensure Success

These principles can maximize success, enhance programs, and position your organization for long-term financial health.

Strategic financial management should be viewed as a vehicle for enhancing service to clients, improving programs, and meeting the financial responsibilities of people who plan conferences, workshops, and meetings. This chapter identifies seven principles for achieving success in the design and implementation of a comprehensive strategic financial planning system. Basic premises underlying all the principles are that a strategic financial management system should complement and support all other types of planning, it should be easy to learn, and it should enhance the overall problem-solving ability of the staff so that they can better serve the organization.

Principle 1: Strategic
Financial Management Should Form
the Foundation for All Organizational Planning

Strategic financial management is a synergistic, ongoing process designed to continually improve the management of the organization's finances. It forms the foundation for all other types of planning and strategy development and affects many other activities related to daily leadership. Thus, strategic financial management can be a major catalyst for change.

Because strategic financial management affects all aspects of organizational planning and leadership, it is important to give a great deal of thought, care, and attention to the design and implementation of a comprehensive strategic financial management system. When properly carried out, strategic financial management clarifies expectations for both short- and long-term budget-management strategies. This requires the involvement of all staff so that everyone understands the relationship of other organizational decisions to financial planning and management. It also requires that only one person should be in charge of a budget for an individual conference, workshop, or meeting.

Strategic financial management is not an isolated event that has a beginning and an end. Rather, it is a flexible, constantly changing process for bringing excellence to all aspects of the organization. When it is most successful, strategic financial management is woven into the daily fabric of organizational life.

Principle 2: A Plan Should Include
Specific Goals and Measurable Objectives

Goals are broad, generalized statements that set direction for future activities. Objectives are subsets of goals. When objectives are properly conceived, they are specific enough to be measured by some agreed-on method, they can be delegated to particular individuals for implementation, and deadlines can be established for achieving them. The following goals and objectives were written for the department of training and development of a national professional association that holds fifty conferences, workshops, and meetings a year for its membership:

Goal

> To have the Department of Training and Development break even each year according to the budget that is negotiated between the director of the department and the executive director of the association.

Objectives

- By March 1, to develop individual budgets for all programs scheduled during the next fiscal year. Sandra will be in charge of ensuring that this happens.

- To review and update each program budget every thirty days from the time it is created until the program has been closed out with all income received and all expenses paid. Sandra will be in charge of implementing this.

- To integrate individual program budget summaries into a master electronic spreadsheet showing the following:
  - Total income
  - Total expenses
  - Administrative fee cost recovery
  - Additional positive or negative balances
  - Net balance for each program after all expenses, including administrative fees, have been paid

  Mark will be in charge of achieving this objective.

The basic premise of strategic financial management is that specific goals and measurable objectives positively affect all aspects of budgeting and financial management. The expectations for financial success are defined and agreed on before any conference, workshop, or meeting is undertaken. No agreements are final until the budget has been agreed to by all key parties. The budget clearly spells out the number of people required to break even, identifies maximum expenses in each budget category, and provides for an appropriate miscellaneous amount to account for unforeseen expenses. Such clarification of financial goals and development of measurable objectives to achieve these goals reduce ambiguity in the organization.

Principle 3: Financial Resource Allocation Creates Policy

Budgeting is the method used to allocate financial resources for a specific account entity: an individual conference, workshop, or meeting or general office expenses. The budgeting process and the strategic financial management underlying that process often create policy. Thus, strategic financial planning can become a powerful tool for either change or maintenance of the status quo. Considerable conflict often emerges as a result of resource allocation and the policies that it creates (Shipp, 1982; Garner, 1991). The following examples illustrate some ways in which the allocation of financial resources creates policy.

Our first example concerns a large university with a completely self-supporting continuing education division that plans many conferences, workshops, meetings, and noncredit classes. The university administration decides to tax all continuing education program income at the rate of 4 percent to fund endowed professorships that are not related to outreach activities.

In response to publicity about the creation of endowed professorships and their high salaries, the community puts pressure on the university administration to offer scholarships to low-income people who cannot afford to attend many of the conferences, workshops, meetings, and noncredit classes. However, because the continuing education office already charges high registration fees in order to remain self-supporting, it cannot offer these scholarships and still ensure a balanced budget when the new 4 percent tax is imposed.

The evening newspaper begins a series of unfavorable stories regarding the institution's lack of responsiveness to the social needs of the community. As a result, the administration insists that continuing education become more responsive to community pressures. The dean of continuing education suggests that the 4 percent tax be allocated for scholarships. The administration refuses and continues to allocate the money to fund the endowed professorships. In making this decision, the institution has clearly stated its value system and priorities and thus has created new policy.

Or consider this example. Because of tight finances, a large museum needs to reduce its budget by $50,000 for the coming year. The director and board of trustees decide to eliminate two positions in the museum's department of education, whose mission is to conduct school tours, evening lectures, seminars, and workshops for a wide variety of community groups within the state.

In the past, all positions in the department of education have been fully funded, and the department has never charged any fees for its programs. Since the department has not planned during good times for any cost recovery, it does not have enough lead time during the current financial crisis to implement the type of cost recovery that will net $50,000 and thus has no option other than to eliminate the two positions. The result is that the department must cut back on many of its programs for public school children.

These two brief examples illustrate how decisions about the allocation of resources often dramatically affect policy. Because of this relationship between allocation of financial resources and policy formation, it is important to approach each with thoughtful problem solving and strategy formation.

Principle 4: Strategy Formation Is an Important Function of Organizational Leadership

Probably no other aspect of leadership is more important than financial strategy development. Written long-range plans that do not include specific financial strategies to implement them are rarely effective. Therefore, an important leadership activity for all staff is the constant development of strategies to ensure that programs, products, and services continue to meet client needs. Without this, organizations tend to move quickly into decline.

There are a number of important issues that leaders should constantly address in relation to strategy development: How can our conferences, workshops, and meetings be designed to best serve the needs of our clients? How should we position our programs in the market to distinguish our organization from providers of similar programs? What opportunities will we have in the future? What are our weaknesses, and how can we best address them? What should be changed about our financial planning to create the best possible financial health for our organization? Addressing these important issues will enhance overall strategy development regarding all financial issues.

Principle 5: Adequate Time Is Necessary to Ensure Success in Strategic Financial Management

Designing and implementing a strategic financial management system and ensuring that strategic financial management becomes an integral part of the daily fabric of organizational life take time. Once a strategic financial management system is in place, it demands constant attention, discussion, analysis, and fine tuning to ensure that it achieves what it was designed to achieve. Therefore, it is important for leaders to carve out adequate time from their busy schedules to address strategic financial management issues. The easiest way to accomplish this is to make appointments with yourself. Each week, allocate specific blocks of time to implement the component parts of your strategic financial management system. For example, you might block out times on your appointment calendar to work on items such as the following:

> Monday, 3:00–4:40 P.M.: Develop on an electronic spreadsheet the final draft of the budget for Workshop on Gerontology.
> Wednesday, 8:30–9:30 A.M.: Review all bills for Workshop on Time Management. Goal: to have a printout of the final budget wrap-up with all encumbrances two weeks after this program is over.
> Thursday, 8:30–9:30 A.M.: Develop the first draft of the budget for the Seminar on Drug-Free Schools to present to the planning committee.
> Friday, 3:00–5:00 P.M.: Review budgets for all programs that are not officially closed out and update my master spreadsheet summarizing my programs for the year

Once your appointments are made, close the door to all interruptions. Be sure that your schedule for planning time is adhered to. In the busy lives of people who plan conferences, workshops, and meetings, there is always the temptation to simply react to issues.

Principle 6: Five-Year Spreadsheets
Should Be Updated Every Thirty Days

The system described in this book calls for an updating every
thirty days of the comprehensive office financial plan for conferences, workshops, and meetings. If the main mission of your
office is something other than planning conferences, workshops,
and meetings, you may not need to do this. However, if this
is a major function of your office, it is important to develop a
five-year financial projection, particularly if you must recover
a portion of your office's expenses in the form of administrative
fees, and to update it every thirty days.

If your office is a unit of a larger parent organization, the
thirty-day update should coincide with the monthly printouts
that you probably receive from the central accounting office.
Reviewing each accounting entity every thirty days makes it
possible to maintain tight control on accounting for all income
and expenses. This assumes that you implement the system of
encumbrances described in this book to account for income that
is expected and expenses that will have to be paid even though
actual bills may not have been received and implement fund
accounting to accurately track income and expenses for individual account entities.

Principle 7: Teams of Problem Solvers Should Be Created

Strategic financial management is not the job only of the director of an office; it is the job of all staff members. Therefore,
it is important to involve staff in designing and implementing
a comprehensive strategic financial planning system. This helps
to create teams of problem solvers, encourages all staff to develop a psychological commitment to the organization, its goals,
and objectives, and mobilizes the expertise and best thinking
of the entire staff.

The financial records should be open to all staff so that
they can conceptualize the entire financial management system
for the office and develop appropriate strategies to enhance its

success. Keeping the budget planning process secret does not promote team problem solving. Open discussion of all aspects of income and expense items for general office expenses will encourage everyone to become responsible for the financial health of the office and to bring their best creative ideas and problem-solving skills to make comprehensive strategic financial management a success. Ownership of ideas, successes, and failures will be shared by the group. This open problem-solving process will maximize the success of a comprehensive strategic financial management system.

Summary

The seven guidelines discussed in this chapter should be individualized in ways that are appropriate for your organization. Implementing these guidelines can maximize success, enhance programs, and position your organization for long-term financial health through the establishment of a comprehensive strategic financial management system.

9.

Leadership Skills
for Strategic Financial Management

> With external pressures increasing in all organi-
> zations, special leadership skills are required to
> implement strategic financial management.

Leadership in all organizations is becoming more complex. The
rapid rate of change has made it difficult for many large organizations to respond to the new expectations and demands of
their clients. Today's hot topics in the world of conferences,
workshops, and meetings may be out of vogue tomorrow. These
rapid shifts in consumer demands and expectations can dramatically affect an organization's financial planning. How do leaders
create the vision to assist their organizations to navigate through
these difficult issues? What kind of skills are needed to achieve
success with strategic financial management in a time of rapid
change? This chapter identifies and analyzes the major skills
needed by leaders who work with conferences, workshops, and
meetings if they are to effectively implement a comprehensive
strategic financial management system.

Managing Ambiguity

The increasingly rapid rate of change in society means that yesterday's solutions to organizational problems often do not apply to today's new issues. We can no longer rely on looking through the rear-view mirror to match yesterday's historically successful solutions to today's problems. Many of the problems we face today simply have no historical precedent. This causes ambiguity to increase at exponential rates in our organizations. And when ambiguity increases, individuals' uncertainty increases.

This presents leaders with a major problem. Because most people feel uncomfortable and uncertain with ambiguity, we tend to gear our daily behavior to reducing ambiguity. However, we probably will be unsuccessful if we simply try to eliminate ambiguity in our organizations. Therefore, we must develop specific strategies for dealing with ambiguity.

We can learn to become successful at managing ambiguity. Action-oriented approaches to managing ambiguity are more successful than laissez-faire ones. The guidelines and principles presented in this book represent action-oriented strategies for managing ambiguity. The emphasis is on asking all staff to take control of their personal and organizational success by reaching clear understandings with supervisors regarding expectations for meeting financial goals. When staff see developing a comprehensive strategic financial management system as one of their main job responsibilities, they immediately take control over managing the ambiguity in their organization.

Engaging in Strategic Long-Range Planning

Strategic long-range planning is a process that gives attention to designing, implementing, and monitoring plans for improving decision making in organizations (Simerly and Associates, 1987). It is concerned with developing an organizational mission statement that reflects the organization's basic value structure. An integral part of this is getting agreement from key stakeholders, such as staff and superiors, on the directions that the origination should take. In addition, it is important to find ways to quantify and measure the effectiveness of actions taken to reach goals and objectives. Finally, a successful process requires revising plans as necessary to account for changing conditions in the environment. Thus, strategic long-range planning is a constantly changing process that concentrates on helping organizations adapt and renew themselves.

Creating a Vision of Successful Strategic Financial Management

Leadership demands vision to guide an organization in mobilizing resources to achieve its goals and thus to make positive contributions to society in general. Visions must inspire staff to want to jump on board the train as it moves out of the station. Visions have an inspirational quality about them. They encourage staff to develop a strong personal commitment to the organization and its future.

One of the chief skills required of leaders involved with planning conferences, workshops, and meetings is the ability to create a vision of where their organization should be headed and how strategic financial management can assist the organization in achieving its overall mission. For example, a manager might say that the mission of an office is to produce a balanced budget. However, a leader would realize that this is not a particularly inspirational vision and would assist the office in reconceptualizing it. The following are examples of mission statements representing visions that go beyond just managing finances successfully:

- For an office of conferences and institutes in the division of continuing education at a university: "The mission of the Office of Conferences and Institutes is to develop programs that mirror the institutional strengths of the university and help meet the lifelong learning needs of society."
- For an office of training and development in a large, for-profit computer software business: "The mission of the Office

of Training and Development is to enhance the quality of work life so our business can help society solve important problems through the use of computer software technology."

- For the department of education in a large historical museum: "The mission of the Department of Education is to plan educational activities that assist society in understanding and appreciating the role history plays in interpreting past and present events."

Leaders are able to see windows of opportunity where others see stumbling blocks to progress. Creating a vision of how strategic financial management should operate in an organization is essential to successful leadership.

Using Stratonomics Effectively

Stratonomics is the concept that the process used for decision making in an organization is just as important as the actual decisions themselves (Simerly, 1990). Leaders in the world of conferences, workshops, and meetings who are concerned with stratonomics will need to spend as much time creating effective processes for decision making regarding strategic financial management as they do in actually making decisions. Another way of saying this is that the way we go about doing tasks is just as important as the tasks themselves. Thus, developing an effective leadership style is critical to personal and organizational success.

The guidelines and principles presented in the case studies in this book emphasize the leader's responsibility for using stratonomics. Throughout the analysis of the issues presented in the cases, there is an emphasis on the importance of the process used to implement strategic financial management. Staff are actively involved in identifying problems in their financial management as well as in designing solutions to those problems.

Engaging in Environmental Scanning

Environmental scanning is a system for identifying movements, trends, and change-producing ideas before they become part of the generally accepted common knowledge base in society. Organizations seeking to be on the cutting edge of these new ideas, trends, and movements need to develop a systematic way to constantly monitor or scan the environment so that new ideas can be translated into new programs (Nadler and Nadler, 1987). Long-term success in strategic financial management requires constantly creating new conferences, workshops, and meetings before the competition does. Thus, leaders need to strive to be first in the market with new program ideas. Entering a market that is already saturated with similar programs can lead to financial disaster. Or, as the sage Yogi Berra said, "If people don't want to come, you can't stop them."

Strategic financial management is not an activity independent of program planning, marketing, staff development, or the many other activities that take place in an organization that plans conferences, workshops, and meetings. Rather, strategic financial management is part of a symbiotic relationship within the organization. Establishing an effective environmental scanning system for new program ideas is essential to long-term success in strategic management.

Managing Conflict for Productive Results

We often hear the term *conflict resolution* used in today's organizations. However, in many ways, this is a dysfunctional term. Conflict resolution implies that you can somehow "resolve" conflict so that it no longer exists. In most organizations, this is an unrealistic and inappropriate approach.

Therefore, we need to reconceptualize our approaches to dealing with conflict. We need to view conflict as a natural and inevitable part of organizational life. Indeed, conflict has many positive aspects. For example, one of the chief motivators of change is conflict related to preserving versus changing the status quo. Dissatisfaction produces conflict, and dealing with conflict often results in change.

One of the most important skills that leaders need to successfully implement a comprehensive strategic financial management system is the ability to manage conflict for productive results. This type of conflict management relieves people of the unconscious obligation to "resolve" conflict so that it does not rear its head again and enables them to view it as a natural and inevitable part of organizational life.

Leaders who plan conferences, workshops, and meetings realize that when planning committees balk at cost recovery through administrative fee charge-backs, this is a natural and inevitable type of conflict that can be managed for productive results.

Using Computer Software for Financial Modeling

The software now available for use with personal computers makes it possible for everyone to easily engage in sophisticated financial modeling. Financial modeling creates alternative financial scenarios and enables people to project the budgetary consequences of these scenarios on electronic spreadsheets to see how different decisions would affect an office's overall financial management.

Using financial software packages to engage in sophisticated financial modeling does not require special accounting or computer skills. The two most popular software programs for this purpose are Lotus 1-2-3 and Excel. Both are available in IBM-compatible and Apple Macintosh versions. With recent developments making these software packages more user friendly, learning them is fast and easy. For example, someone with no experience using electronic spreadsheets can easily learn how to program all the budget forms and financial scenarios used in the case studies in this book in a morning or an afternoon.

Once you have learned how to program these electronic spreadsheets, it is important to carve out enough time to create the kinds of models appropriate to your individual situation. The forms and printouts in this book can easily be modified to meet individual needs. Adapting, designing, and programming all the different types of printouts recommended in this book should take less than a day for most offices that plan even a large number of conferences, workshops, and meetings.

Conducting Sophisticated Market Research

Effective strategic financial management and effective marketing are directly related to each other. *Marketing* can be defined as establishing effective two-way communication between an organization and its publics. With this definition, advertising and public relations are subsets of marketing. *Advertising* refers to any form of paid communication; *public relations* refers to any form of nonpaid communication (Simerly and Associates, 1989).

The best budgets in the world will not be successful if an organization does not constantly engage in sophisticated market research. A number of questions need to be answered by anyone engaging in market research: What program topics are in most demand by the people we serve with our conferences, workshops, and meetings? How do we know this? Historically, how many people register for every thousand brochures we mail to advertise programs? Answering this last question requires accurate tracking systems for tracing individual registrants to specific mailing lists (Prisk, 1989; Simerly, 1990a).

It is also important to ask whether programs are priced correctly in relation to what customers expect to pay for a registration fee. This often varies from group to group. For example, physicians often will not register for low-priced workshops because they equate higher prices with higher quality. On the other hand, nurses often have to pay either part or all of the registration fee for workshops themselves. Therefore, this segment of the market will often reject high registration fees.

When is the best time of the year to hold each program? What days of the week are most convenient for registrants? How long should each program last? These questions show that an excellent strategic financial management system must be supported by equally excellent market research. Market research forms the foundation on which all strategic financial management should rest.

Developing Research-Based Marketing Plans

The purpose of sophisticated market research is to develop detailed marketing plans for each conference, workshop, and meeting. Each plan should have the following characteristics. First, it should be research-based. Marketing plans based on hunches can be risky. Second, it should include careful analysis of the data that it produces. Third, it should include research into the pricing of programs and the number of people that can be expected to register. Fourth, it should indicate how far in advance brochures advertising the program should be mailed for each group of potential registrants (Simerly, 1990a).

Developing a detailed data-based marketing plan for each program is just as important as developing a budget for the program. These two items are interdependent and equally necessary for a program to break even.

Simplifying Strategic Financial Management

If it is to be effective throughout the organization, strategic financial management needs to be as simple as possible. The system that you develop should be easily understood by people who have never had an accounting course. Therefore, it is important to create a glossary of terms that will be used when referring to financial issues and distribute it to the staff. Training sessions can help staff members to learn the terms and how they are used in daily problem solving.

There should also be an obvious logic behind all data presentations. The budget forms presented in this book can be modified to meet the needs of any organization that plans conferences, workshops, and meetings. Regardless of the size of a program, its complexity, or who sponsors it, the logic of presenting the data related to budgeting and strategic financial management remains the same.

This also holds true for the spreadsheets presenting data on the entire fiscal year for an office and all its programs. Staff members need to have access to these data and to be trained to understand the meaning of the terms that are used each day when strategic financial management is discussed. The major financial management terms used in this book are summarized in Resource B. When the language is kept simple and the number of terms small, it is easy for staff members who have never had an accounting course — and those who suffer from math anxiety — to become skilled at strategic financial management.

Bring Continuous Improvements to
the Strategic Financial Management System

Continuous quality improvement means that the strategic financial management system in an office has been designed to give staff and consumers the best possible service. Therefore, an excellent strategic financial management system should be designed to ask "What if?" questions. With the answers to these questions, financial models can be developed on spreadsheets — models that attempt to capture the dynamic variables that operate in the real world. This enables staff to analyze the financial consequences of different scenarios before any decisions actually have to be made.

The system should be flexible enough to adapt to the impact of a rapidly changing environment on the entire operation of an office. This is why it is essential to review all individual program budgets every thirty days at least. This review should provide a series of checks and balances so that early warning signals alert staff to potential problems. In addition, the system should be updated every twenty-four hours so all individual budgets for conferences, workshops, and meetings are accurate. Anything less is to settle for a less than optimum strategic financial management system.

Continuous quality improvement, if it is to be successful, is not just the job of the top person in an office. It should become the responsibility of all staff. In order to establish this kind of commitment to designing, implementing, and maintaining a comprehensive strategic financial management system, all staff need to understand the role they each play in making the system work.

Summary

This chapter has reviewed the skills that leaders need to be effective in designing and implementing strategic financial management. Once a strategic financial management system has been successfully implemented, it needs constant attention and fine tuning to ensure that it remains responsive to the needs of staff as well as clients. New strategies and techniques for improving financial management must constantly be developed and tested. Strategic financial management is not an action that has a beginning and an end. It is an ongoing process that should be woven into the daily fabric of organizational life.

Resource A.
Sample
Budget Forms

The three sample forms included in this resource demonstrate the great flexibility possible in the development of budget forms for a wide variety of conferences, workshops, and meetings.

Budget form 1, presented in Exhibit A.1, is a basic program budget form used in many of the illustrations in this book. When this budget form is programmed on an electronic spreadsheet, it can easily be modified to meet individual program needs. This short budget form can become the basis for longer budget forms that may be required for larger, more complex programs. Note that fixed and variable expenses are always clearly separated on the form.

Budget form 2, presented in Exhibit A.2, illustrates how to expand budget form 1 to account for additional expenses. This budget form has been filled out to illustrate the clarity with which data are displayed. Fixed and variable expenses are clearly separated. The category for instructors' travel, per diem, honoraria, and other expenses has been expanded to provide more detailed data. A section for "sunk costs"—up-front expenses that are incurred even if a program is canceled—has been added. By clearly identifying these, you can quickly figure out whether you will lose more by holding the program or canceling it if the number of registrations does not reach the break-even point. Like the other budget forms, this one can easily be programmed on an electronic spreadsheet.

At first glance, budget form 3 (Exhibit A.3) appears to be very different from the previous forms. In reality, however, it is very similar to the others, even though it displays data differently. As in the other forms, fixed and variable expenses are clearly separated. "Sunk costs" are identified. Thus, if the program fails to secure its break-even number of registrants, it will be easy to figure out whether you will lose more money by holding the program or canceling it.

This longer form is useful for beginning discussions of expense items in planning committee meetings. While it is unlikely that a program will incur every expense listed, this comprehensive list helps guide discussions. Like the other forms, this one can also be easily programmed on an electronic spreadsheet.

Exhibit A.1. Budget Form 1.

Fixed expenses		Per person variable expenses	
Presenters			
Honorarium		Registration packet	
Fringe benefits		Food	
Travel			
Advertising			
Printing			
Graphic design			
Typesetting			
Mailing			
Additional ads			
Mailing list rental			
Administrative		Total per person variable expenses	
Administrative fee			
Materials/supplies			
Duplicating			
General expenses			
Complimentary registrations			
Subtotal fixed expenses			
Divided by			
to break even			
Add total per person variable expenses			
Subtotal			
Add 10% miscellaneous			
Subtotal			
Add % credit card fee			
Total expenses per person		**Registration fee per person**	

Exhibit A.2. Budget Form 2.

Account number:	385				
Program title:	Negotiating Global Trade Agreements				
Dates:	July 4–7				
Location:	Washington, D.C.				
Program manager;	Thomas West				
Payroll/travel					
Instructors	Travel	Per diem	Honorarium	Other	
Margaret Smithson	$ 1,584.00	$200	$2,000	$175	
Thomas Melbourne	687.00	100	500	75	
Judith Wayson	837.00	225	1,500	80	
Max Radder	786.00	100	1,500	90	
Leanne Wilcox	1,639.00	200	2,000	180	
Totals	$ 5,533.00	$825	$7,500	$600	
Subtotal above	$14,458.00				
section					
Fixed expenses			**Per person variable**		
			expenses		
Administrative travel	$689.00		Registration pack	$ 12	
Administrative fee	$10,000.00		Notebook	8	
Entertainment	$800.00		Paper/pencils	3	
Photography	$500.00		Two lunches @ $25	50	
Equipment rental	$800.00		Two dinners @ $45	90	
Equipment moving	$575.00				
Security	$890.00		Totals	$163	
General duplicating	$1,589.00				
Publicity	$2,500.00				
Complimentary expenses—					
10 @ $163 each	$1,630.00				
Graphic design	900.00				
Typesetting	$390.00				
List rental	$5,500.00				
Advertising	$2,000.00				
Printing—75,000					
brochures @ $.35 each	$26,250.00				

Exhibit A.2. Budget Form 2, Cont'd.

Mailing and handling				
75,000 brochures				
@ $.25 each	$18,750.00			
Subtotal	$88,221.00			
Plus 10% miscellaneous	8,822.00			
Subtotal	$97,043.00			
Divided by 500				
people to break		**Sunk Costs**		
even	194.00	Publicity		$ 2,500
Total fixed costs		Duplicating		500
per person	194.00	Graphic design		900
Total variable costs		Typesetting		390
per person	163.00	List rental		5,500
Subtotal	$357.00	Advertising		2,000
Credit card fee @ 3.5%	12.50	Printing		26,250
Total per person		Mailing/handling		18,750
expenses	$369.50			
Registration fee	$370.00	**Total**		$56,790
		These are the costs that will be		
		incurred if the program must		
		be canceled.		

Exhibit A.3. Budget Form 3.

Part 1—Per person variable expenses			
1. Food service	Amount		
_____breakfasts @ _____			
_____lunches @ _____			
_____dinners @ _____			
_____breaks @ _____			
_____social hours @ _____			
Other			
Subtotal			
Tax @ _____ %			
Subtotal			
Gratuity @ _____ %			
Food subtotal			
2. Printed materials			
Registration packets			
Notebooks			
Per person duplicating			
Paper/pencils			
Proceedings			
Other			
Subtotal			
3. Other per person variable costs			
Per person administrative fee			
Other			
4. Total variable costs per person			

Exhibit A.3. Budget Form 3, Cont'd.

Part 2 — Preprogram expenses			
(sunk costs)	Amount		
5. Printing			
Announcements			
Brochures			
Posters			
Flyers			
Other			
Subtotal			
6. Mailing			
List rental			
Postage			
Handling			
Other			
Subtotal			
7. Advertising			
Publicity releases			
Ads			
Other			
Subtotal			
8. Planning meetings			
Travel			
Meals			
Refreshments			
Hotel			
Other			
Subtotal			
9. Other expenses			
Subtotal			
10. Total part 2 (lines 5–9)			

Exhibit A.3. Budget Form 3, Cont'd.

Part 3 — Program expenses	Amount		
11. Instructors			
Name	Honoraria	Travel	Other
Subtotal			
12. Fringe benefits			
Fringes @ _____ % of all honoraria			
13. Instructional materials			
Books			
Handouts			
General duplicating			
Other			
Subtotal			
14. Rentals			
Audiovisual equipment			
Films/tapes			
Space			
Other			
Subtotal			
15. General transportation			
Bus			
Car			
Other			
Subtotal			
16. Graphics			
Graphic design			
Typesetting			
Other			
Subtotal			

Exhibit A.3. Budget Form 3, Cont'd.

	Amount		
17. Other expenses			
Photography			
Moving			
Signs			
Certificates			
Phones			
Flowers			
Exhibit space rental			
Cost sharing			
Subtotal			
18. Complimentary registrations			
_____ people @ _____			
Part 4 — Summary information			
Subtotal all fixed expenses			
Total fixed expenses divided by _____ people			
to break even			
Total fixed expenses per person			
Total variable expenses per person			
Subtotal			
Add _____ % for miscellaneous			
Subtotal			
Add credit card fee @ _____ %			
Total expenses per person			
Registration fee			

Resource B.
Important
Financial Management Terms

This resource summarizes the major financial terms used in this book. The definitions indicate how these terms are used in financial planning for conferences, workshops, and meetings.

Accrual accounting: an accounting method that treats money as income when it is earned, even though it may not actually have been received, and money to be paid out as an expense whenever bills are incurred, even though they may not actually have been received or paid. This is the most effective accounting method for the strategic financial management of conferences, workshops, and meetings.

Administrative cost recovery: the process through which general overhead expenses that are difficult to assign to individual programs are prorated and charged back to individual conferences, workshops, and meetings through separate fees. There are four major methods of administrative cost recovery. With the flat administrative fee method, a fixed dollar amount is charged to each program in the form of an administrative fee. The *per person variable fee* method establishes a per person dollar amount of the registration fee to be recovered for overhead. The *percentage of total expenses* method charges a flat percentage of the total expenses. The *combination* method often offers the most flexibility but is also the most complex and time-consuming to administer.

Budgeting: the process of creating documents (budgets) that project income and expenses in relation to individual account entities.

Cash accounting: an accounting method that treats money as income only when it is received and money going out of the organization as an expense only when bills are actually paid. This method is most often found in large, centralized accounting offices in a parent organization. It works very well for stewardship accounting. However, it is not helpful with the daily management of finances for individual offices and their respective programs and thus is not suitable for managing conferences, workshops, and meetings.

Encumbrance: the formal way of noting the exact dollar amount of any income that is expected (even though the money may not actually have been received) or any expense that is to be paid (even though the bill may not have been received). When money is encumbered on a balance sheet, the exact dollar amounts of all expected income and expenses are listed under separate codes. When expected income is actually received or expected expenses are actually paid, the encumbrance code is removed, and the posting stands as an actual income or expense. This is a very helpful system for maintaining an accurate record of how a budget is doing for any individual program.

Fixed expenses: program expenses that will remain constant no matter how many people attend. For example, the costs of printing and mailing brochures to advertise a program are fixed expenses. No matter how many people attend, these expenses will have been incurred far in advance of the event and will not change.

Fund accounting: a system for dividing the money for an entire office into appropriate separate accounts. Each account has its own account code, so income and expenses related to that particular fund can be easily tracked. Income and expenses from separate programs or funds are never commingled.

General overhead expenses: general expenses incurred in running an office that cannot easily be attributed to a specific program. For example, utilities, insurance, maintenance, and equipment purchases are usually considered general overhead expenses.

Stewardship accounting: the formal accounting system used by many large organizations. Six to twelve months after a program has been held, stewardship accounting can demonstrate that income was received and expenses paid according to the guidelines and laws governing the organization. Stewardship accounting is not usually designed to assist with daily financial management by providing a daily record of income and expenses that have been posted to an account within the last twenty-four hours. Rather, it is intended to meet an organization's legal obligation to demonstrate after the fact that it was a good steward, or protector, of funds.

Strategic financial management: the development of specific strategies to ensure the overall financial health of a budget or series of budgets over a period of time.

Variable expenses: expenses that will vary depending on how many people attend a program. For example, food is a variable expense.

Resource C.
Helpful
Personal Computer Software

The budget forms presented in this book can easily be programmed on electronic spreadsheets for personal computers. Although there are many different spreadsheet software packages available, Excel and Lotus 1-2-3 are the leaders in the field. They are both user friendly and versatile. Both Lotus 1-2-3 and Excel offer updated versions approximately every two years. Be sure to get the latest version, which will always be more user friendly and contain the latest enhancements.

There are also a number of software packages that can be used for complete meeting management, enabling you to easily handle the many details associated with conferences, workshops, and meetings. An integral part of these software packages is a budget preparation and management module. Although these modules are not designed to handle all the types of spreadsheet applications found in this book, they are useful for many financial planning and management tasks. Typically, these software packages provide an integrated way to prepare budgets, name badges, personalized confirmation letters, reports, mailing lists, certificates, and rosters. The following are the three best software packages. As with all software programs, it is important to examine them carefully to determine whether they meet your individual needs.

Peopleware
1621 114th Avenue, S.E.
Suite 120
Bellevue, WA 98004
(800) 869-7166

Meeting Ware
383 East
1800 South
Orem, Utah 84058
(801) 226-5226

Logic Resources, Inc.
Heart Business Center
P.O. Box 7765
Peace River, Alberta
Canada T8S 1T3
(403) 624-8666 or
(800) 663-1797

References

Garner, W. C. *Accounting and Budgeting in Public and Nonprofit Organizations: A Manager's Guide.* San Francisco: Jossey-Bass, 1991.

Hildreth, R. A. *The Essentials of Meeting Management.* Englewood Cliffs, N.J.: Prentice Hall, 1990.

Matkin, G. W. *Effective Budgeting in Continuing Education: A Comprehensive Guide to Improving Program Planning and Organizational Performance.* San Francisco: Jossey-Bass, 1985.

Nadler, L., and Nadler, Z. *The Comprehensive Guide to Successful Conferences and Meetings: Detailed Instructions and Step-by-Step Checklists.* San Francisco: Jossey-Bass, 1987.

Prisk, D. P. "Budgeting for Marketing Activities and Staff Costs." In R. G. Simerly and Associates, *Handbook of Marketing for Continuing Education.* San Francisco: Jossey-Bass, 1989.

Shipp, T. (ed.). *Creative Financing and Budgeting.* New Directions for Continuing Education, no. 16. San Francisco: Jossey-Bass, 1982.

Simerly, R. G. *Planning and Marketing Conferences and Workshops: Tips, Tools, and Techniques.* San Francisco: Jossey-Bass, 1990a.

Simerly, R. G. "Stratonomics: Ten Important Leadership Issues for Continuing Education." In *Personnel: Conferences and Institutes Resource Book 1990.* Washington, D.C.: National University Continuing Education Association, 1990b.

Simerly, R. G., and Associates. *Strategic Planning and Leadership in Continuing Education: Enhancing Organizational Vitality, Responsiveness, and Identity.* San Francisco: Jossey-Bass, 1987.

Simerly, R. G., and Associates. *Handbook of Marketing for Continuing Education.* San Francisco: Jossey-Bass, 1989.

Wagner, R. *Fee Management for Noncredit Programs.* Manhattan, Kans.: Learning Resources Network, 1981.

Index

A

Access of budget data, 21; for budget balancing, 78; of comprehensive office, 25-26, 85-86; for daily decision making, 45, 47, 94. *See also* Budget forms; Display

Account codes, 53, 65, 109. *See also* Fund accounting

Accounting system: concepts for, 49-54; for daily decision making, 43-54; for effective strategic financial management, 4; need for simplification of, 94; for office budget, 25. *See also* Accrual accounting; Cash accounting; Centralized accounting; Fund accounting

Accrual accounting: case study of, 50-52; vs. cash accounting, 49-52; defined, 49-50, 107; establishment of, 49-52, 53; example of, 65; sample form for, 52

Administrative cost recovery, 81, 83; and budget balancing, 71; case study of, 33-40; and conflict, 92; defined, 107-108; for effective strategic financial management, 4; methods for, 34-40, 41-42; by program director, 66, 68; record-keeping system for, 58; in sample form, 64, 65. *See also* General overhead expenses

Advertising, 93, 94. *See also* Marketing

Ambiguity, management of, 88